Planning Corporate Manpower

Management Studies Series

under the editorship of E. F. L. Brech, B.A., B.Sc.(Econ.), F.B.I.M.

Integrated Managerial Controls (second edition)
R. O. Boyce

Management Diagnosis—A Practical Guide
R. O. Boyce and H. Eisen

Construction Management in Principle and Practice
E. F. L. Brech

Appraising Capital Works
E. J. Broster

Management Statistics
E. J. Broster

Planning Profit Strategies
E. J. Broster

Marketing for Expansion and Europe
C. Godley and D. Cracknell

Personnel Administration and Industrial Relations
J. V. Grant and G. J. Smith

Marketing for Profit (second edition)
L. Hardy

Management Glossary
H. Johannsen and A. B. Robertson

The Economics and Management of System Construction
G. Leon

Management in the Printing Industry
C. Spector

Industrial Marketing Management and Controls
L. A. Williams

Planning Corporate Manpower

D. J. Bell

Longman

658.3
B 433

Longman
1724-1974

LONGMAN GROUP LIMITED
London

*Associated companies, branches and representatives
throughout the world*

© Longman Group Limited 1974

First published 1974

ISBN 0 582 44584 1

Library of Congress Catalog
Card Number: 73-86105

Set in 10/12 pt u/lc Plantin 110
and printed in Great Britain by
Adlard & Son Limited
Bartholomew Press, Dorking, Surrey

Contents

Foreword

The purpose of this book is to explain the concepts of manpower planning and its place in corporate management to managers and, in particular, personnel managers, who have not done detailed work in this field. In trying to do this, I decided that it was necessary briefly to explain the techniques being used and developed in manpower planning. Managers should, I believe, have an understanding of what is being done by the 'experts', even if they do not need to be able to carry out the detailed work themselves. Too often we attribute to our own superiors an inability to understand what we are doing: this conveniently absolves us from ever explaining the elements of it, but, more significantly, inhibits their ability to make rational and well-informed decisions. Ultimately, manpower planning is concerned with management decisions about manpower and, indeed, about other resources, so that management should understand the context of their decisions and the basis of the information and advice which they are offered to help them make them.

Because of this treatment, the book may be useful to those beginning on manpower planning as a specialism, but, since this is not intended to be a complete textbook on the subject, they are urged to extend their studies into the more expert work of others, much of which is referred to in this book.

The number of people whom I should thank are too many to mention. I sometimes wonder how many ideas authors have themselves, and how many are derived from the ideas of others. Often, if you have accepted someone else's idea, it is difficult to remember that it was not your own. If you have adopted and then adapted an idea, it becomes almost impossible to remember. Nevertheless, although many of the ideas in this book derive from others, the responsibility for it rests with me, for good or ill, and not with those whose ideas I have used.

Some, however, I must single out for thanks. My employers, United Dominions Trust Ltd, have not objected to a part of my energies going on this book, and some ideas stem from my work there. Other ideas were developed while I worked at the Central Electricity Generating Board, Gillette Industries Ltd and International Computers Ltd. There are references in the text to the published work of many individuals, but I must add to these certain people with whom I have worked on manpower problems: Annette Gold and Pauline Brunt, who worked with me in a small manpower planning team at ICL and some of whose work is incorporated into the ideas set out in this book; Jimmy Greer, who was briefly my manager before I left ICL; and Ron Harrison, who once worked on a project in association with me. The discussions, formal and informal, with my colleagues in the Manpower Society have been invaluable, and it was my fellow-members of the Edinburgh Group who first stimulated my interest in manpower planning and who have helped me greatly, both through the manpower planning and computerised personnel information system studies.

Finally, I must thank Margaret Brooks, who typed the whole book for me and helped to keep me writing, aided in the latter by my wife, who withstood the absorption of my leisure time for more than two years.

DAVID BELL

Acknowledgements

We are grateful to the following for permission to reproduce copyright material:

E. F. L. Brech for a quote from *Managing for Revival*, Management Publications Ltd, for B.I.M. London, 1972; Gower Press Ltd, for extracts from *Personnel Review* 1.1 Autumn, 1971, by A. R. Smith; I. G. Helps for a table and an extract from his paper, *Craft Manpower Planning*, 1968; Her Majesty's Stationery Office for an extract from *CAS Occasional Paper 15—Some Statistical Techniques in Manpower Planning* by D. J. Bartholomew; Institute of Personnel Management for an extract from *Perspectives in Manpower Planning* by The Edinburgh Group. © Institute of Personnel Management 1967. Used with permission of the Institute of Personnel Management; Royal Statistical Society and the authors for an extract from 'A method of labour turnover analysis' by K. F. Lane and J. E. Andrews, *JRSS Series A*, **118**, 1955, pp 296–323.

1

The rise of manpower planning

Manpower is a resource. Like financial and material resources, manpower is a necessity for any enterprise. Unlike them, it has been given little planning attention. Relatively sophisticated techniques have been developed to plan expenditure and control it by means of budgetary and accounting systems. Similarly, the use of material resources is planned with care and monitored. Production targets are set and performance is measured against them. Stock control systems have been developed. Sales recording systems are commonplace in marketing firms. Yet manpower planning and control is usually of little apparent concern to management and frequently is neglected altogether.

It is salutary to examine what proportion of the company's revenue expenditure is spent on salaries and wages and the associated overheads of manpower, ranging from insurance contributions to the offices they sit in. In traditionally labour intensive manufacturing industries it can often be more than half, as it may well be also in companies depending on technological advance, such as electronics, which demand fewer, but more expensive, men. Even if it is a much smaller proportion, for example in such industries as chemical manufacture or electricity generation, it is worth considering how crucial to the company's operations manpower is.

THE GENESIS OF MANPOWER PLANNING

The neglect of manpower questions has been common throughout British industry. However, the situation has been changing gradually. This is not so much because the gap in management planning and control has been perceived, but because some of the direct results of the failure to plan and control manpower have been impressing themselves on managements.

1

Firstly, there have been, and still are, shortages of manpower in some skill categories. The notion that manpower need not be planned because it is always available is not always true. Secondly, it has been increasingly obvious that manpower productivity in Britain falls vastly below the standards set by the USA and some other industrialised countries. In a now famous article [1][1] in 1964, William Allen, an American consultant, had drawn attention to figures which, at the very least, allowed the presumption that manpower was not used in Britain to the best advantage. Some of his figures were:

	Britain : USA
Men to produce one ton of steel	3 : 1
Time to build house	3 : 1 to 6 : 1
Maintenance force in chemical industry	4 : 1

Worse still, in spite of Allen's own optimism, the situation is little improved. Figure 1.1 shows that Britain's production per person is less than half the USA's, and well below a number of other countries', including all the Common Market, except Italy. And Italy is gaining. Figure 1.2 shows that the growth rates of many countries, including several who are already ahead, is much greater than Britain's 18 per cent in the period 1964 to mid-1971. In a follow-up article, Keith Richardson also gave some detailed figures [2].

Such figures do not tell the whole story, and must be interpreted with caution. Manpower costs less in Britain than in USA, for example, so that a direct comparison of numbers is not sensible. Such comparisons, however, do show that methods of measuring, planning and controlling manpower productivity may achieve considerable improvements. And certainly such comparisons have given management—rightly or wrongly—the impression that productivity in Britain is poor.

Allied to industry's awareness of the need to improve has been the increasing Government attention to manpower generally and productivity in particular. The activities of the National Board for Prices and Incomes during the period 1965–70, under the Labour administration, repeatedly emphasised the importance of productivity improvement and of measuring it. Successive prices and incomes policies reinforced this. The Conservatives' Industrial Training Act 1964 was also having an increasing effect in the same period. Some of the Industrial Training

[1] Numbers in square brackets relate to references provided at the end of the book, see p. 170.

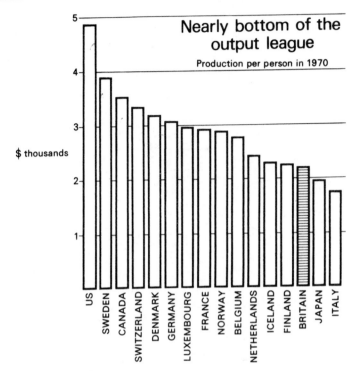

FIG. 1.1   Production per person
(Reproduced from *Sunday Times*, 2 January 1972)

Boards were realising that they had a planning role and that planning training was merely a component part of manpower planning.

Other legislation—Redundancy Payments Act, Contracts of Employment Act and the Selective Employment Tax—was also calling attention to manpower questions. Perhaps more significant than any of these in focusing industry's attention on manpower was the National Plan, 1965 [3], now almost forgotten. In the first place, it called on industry to forecast its manpower needs in 1970, five years ahead. Few of them could. In the few weeks allowed by the Department of Economic Affairs most of them were unable to develop any system to make such forecasts, but some were left with the thought that they should. In the second place, the resultant Plan forecast the 'manpower gap': a shortage of 200,000 in 1970. The impact of this forecast was tempered by the knowledge that the forecast of a 'gap' of less than

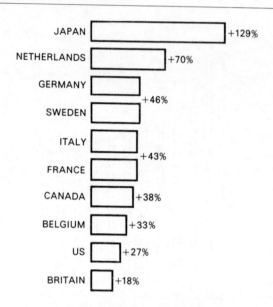

JAPAN +129%

NETHERLANDS +70%

GERMANY +46%

SWEDEN

ITALY +43%

FRANCE

CANADA +38%

BELGIUM +33%

US +27%

BRITAIN +18%

Bottom of the growth league

Based on industrial production from 1964 up to mid-1971

FIG. 1.2   Growth rates
(Reproduced from *Sunday Times*, 2 January 1972)

one per cent of the workforce, based on such suspect forecasts from industry, was inconclusive. Nevertheless it was a danger signal, and the implicit assumption of the National Plan—that the 'gap' could be closed by improved manpower utilisation—led many managements to think about their resource of manpower.

The unsatisfactory nature of the National Plan itself, which owed as much to politics as to planning, had the effect of emphasising what was needed. The very fact that no revisions were forthcoming drew attention in a very clear way to the need to revise and adapt plans constantly. It showed that planning is a continuous adaptive process. The fact that it was not really a plan at all also indicated to industry the need to study planning technique. It was much more a forecast on a given set of assumptions and the planning element—how to bring about what was forecast—was largely missing. Finally, the speed with which the assumptions were disproved, while it may have discredited planning in general in some people's eyes, made others realise that plans could be laid on differing sets of assumptions.

MANPOWER PLANNING 1965–70

Although there was manpower planning work going on in some companies before 1965, it was not until that date that interest grew. On the national front, the Manpower Research Unit had been set up within the then Ministry of Labour. It began its work with tremendous energy with a general forecast of manpower resources, published in 1964 [4], and a series of single industry studies [5], three of which followed within a year. However, the industry studies tended to be exercises in gathering historic data, thorough enough in themselves, but only occasionally were forecasts made.

Gradually, the output of the Unit fell away. Apparently support from the Government was waning. Yet there continued to be great faith in what it could do. The Estimates Committee of the House of Commons in 1967 [6] suggested that each Industrial Training Board required industry by industry forecasts from it. At the rate of production at that time, such a task would have taken more than 30 years.

Government emphasis changed towards the end of the Labour administration from manpower utilisation to industrial relations, and this probably affected the Manpower Research Unit. To the outsider, at least, it seemed that its output decreased even further. Nevertheless in 1970 the national manpower planning task needed for the proper functioning of Industrial Training Boards was again attributed to the Unit by the Frank Cousins's committee reviewing the Central Training Council [7].

Meanwhile, in industry interest in manpower planning was growing. The Institute of Personnel Management published in 1966 a booklet by Dr D. H. Gray, setting out many of the problems [8]. This was followed the next year by another booklet, resulting from a two-year study by the Edinburgh Group of young personnel specialists, which set out the framework of manpower planning needed in industry to tackle the problems, as well as the necessity for supporting Government forecasting [9]. The Manpower Research Unit followed this with a booklet explaining the same framework for company manpower planning [10]. These two booklets remain the best comprehensive handbooks of manpower planning, but they give little detail of the developing techniques. The many papers and articles on these are listed in a bibliography published in 1969 [11], and it is hoped that the Institute of Manpower Studies (see below) will bring this up to date soon.

This bibliography was prepared by a working party under the aegis of a Manpower Planning Study Group of the Operational Research Society. This study group, symbolising the interdisciplinary approach required for manpower planning, was set up in 1967 and received unexpectedly wide support. In 1970, having outgrown its study group status, it became the Manpower Society, sponsored jointly by the OR Society and the Institute of Personnel Management, under the Presidency of Sir William Armstrong, Head of the Home Civil Service. At the same time, J. S. Gough of ICI took over as chairman from A. R. Smith (Civil Service Department). He has now been succeeded by Professor D. J. Bartholomew of the University of Kent at Canterbury.[2] Some of the talks given to the Manpower Society have been published [12].

During this period, the Government had set up the Civil Service Department, directly under Sir William Armstrong's control, one of whose tasks is manpower planning. The services had for some time been doing a considerable amount of manpower planning (see, for example, A. R. Smith's account of the Royal Navy's work [13]). A series of conferences were organised by NATO, including work from civilian life but with a strongly military content: the first took place in 1965 in Brussels [14]. The few firms with any formal manpower planning section were joined by a number of others: many more began to see the need and to search for the means and the staff to fulfil it.

Relevant research was going on in a number of universities. Notably, statistical techniques were being developed by Professor A. Young at Liverpool University (now of the New University of Ulster) and Professor D. J. Bartholomew and his team at the University of Kent at Canterbury. A number of large companies, however, felt the need to give research an added impetus and contributed the funds to set up in 1969 an independent research body, the Institute of Manpower Studies, located at the University of Sussex and the London School of Economics. Its first President was the late Lord Jackson of Burnley, Pro-Rector of the Imperial College, who for several years had been chairman of the Ministry of Technology's Committee on Manpower Resources for Science and Technology. With Vice-Presidents from ICI, the DEP, the TUC and Oxford University, it has broad support.

---

[2] The president is now Lord Fulton and the author is chairman.

This is the context in which manpower planning has grown up. The impetus towards manpower planning seems not always to have been based on a full understanding of what it is and what it aims to achieve and this is the subject of the next chapter.

2

Manpower planning in the company

The resource of manpower has been neglected by managements. Manpower planning aims to fill the gap in their planning and use of resources and thus to avoid shortages and poor utilisation of manpower. Planning resources is not, however, a task which can be done individually for each resource without reference to the others. Manpower costs money and different types of manpower cost different amounts. Increased material resources in the form of machinery might be a substitute for manpower, and this would involve capital investment. Manpower planning must be integrated with other planning work. Equally, other planning work is incomplete without manpower planning.

Thus, the prime objective of manpower planning is to incorporate the planning and control of manpower resources into company planning, so that all resources are used together in the best possible conjunction.

The second objective is to coordinate all company manpower policies. Decisions affecting manpower are continually being made, by line managers and by personnel managers. Recruitment and training programmes, promotion and transfer policies, changes in methods of utilisation or in remuneration, negotiating decisions—all these affect the future need for manpower and its supply. At present, such decisions are made in the absence of any clear means of assessing their effects or their relevance to the objectives of the company. Naturally those who take the decisions have attempted to take all factors into account, but they rarely have the information to do this satisfactorily.

Furthermore, particularly in a large organisation, it is difficult to ensure that the various manpower decisions harmonise with each other. For example, have the implications of a planned change of organisation been thought through so that the recruitment programme is suitably amended? And from there, does the training programme accommodate the changes, and is the salary policy suitably adjusted to attract the staff needed?

To do all this properly, it is necessary to translate the objectives of the company, which are embodied in the change in organisation, into the personnel activities which make them achievable. And to make the translation effectively, considerable analytical work is required. Thus a manpower planning system is needed to achieve this second objective of coordinating manpower policies both with each other and with the company's objectives.

As a result of the achievement of the two objectives, staff costs are reduced, not only through an overall improvement in productivity, but also through the possibility of giving training, recruitment and the other personnel decisions a clearer direction. In addition, the danger of the company's plans being frustrated through not having the right people in the right place at the right time is obviated. Furthermore, management control of manpower resources is increased as a result of the availability of better information and of the systematic use of it.

It seems often to be felt that planning restricts management's freedom of action, but this is a complete misreading of the situation. The availability of information and the means of analysing it ensure that changes can be evaluated. Frequently, a change will be anticipated, thus increasing the time available to make a fully reasoned decision. Nothing is so inflexible as the failure to think ahead, so that changes are never made until they become inevitable. The most appropriate course of action may be precluded because it is too late: certainly the changes are then not fully in management's control.

THE PLANNING METHOD

Manpower planning is the systematic analysis of the company's resources, the construction of a forecast of its future manpower requirements from this base, with special concentration on the efficient use of manpower at both these stages, and the planning necessary to ensure that the manpower supply will match the forecast requirements. To enable the plans to be made, the forecast of requirements must be reconciled with other forecasts—of the supply of manpower from within the company and from without. This definition reveals the five elements of manpower planning:

● Systematic analysis of manpower resources

- Forecast of manpower demand (or requirements)
- Forecast of manpower supply
- Reconciliation within the constraints of the company's circumstances
- Plans for action

It is perhaps worth emphasising the distinction between a forecast, which is a prediction of what will happen on a certain set of assumptions, and a plan, which is an action programme, resulting from the decisions of management based on the forecasts.

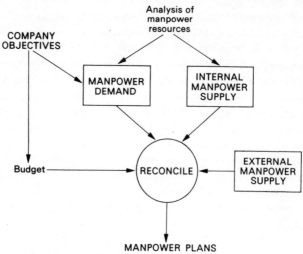

FIG. 2.1   Manpower planning process

MANPOWER FORECASTS

Figure 2.1 shows how the manpower planning method works.

The demand forecast must derive from the objectives of the company, which are set out in the business plan. The analysis of resources provides the means of translating the objectives into manpower terms. To forecast the relationship between the work load of the business plan and the manpower required, analyses of past manpower performance and trends in productivity are needed. If it is to be useful in guiding action, the forecast must also provide information about the types of manpower required: it must be divided into specified manpower categories.

The supply of manpower available from within the company, similarly divided into categories, is forecast on the basis of past rates of staff retention and patterns of promotion and transfer.

These two forecasts will match only in the most exceptional circumstances. It is therefore necessary to consider what actions are necessary to achieve a reconciliation between demand and supply.

Recruitment is the most obvious way of increasing supply. This has to be examined in the light of any constraints which seem likely to be imposed by future labour market conditions. Further information is therefore required here, and in some cases special studies may be needed, so that an external supply forecast can be made.

The reconciliation must also be achieved within constraints imposed by the budget. This, like the demand forecast, stems from the business plan. It may be, however, that when the detailed work has been done the manpower implications of the business plan are found not to be wholly compatible with the financial implications. It may be that financial restrictions limit manpower. In any case the cost of manpower, and of the plans to supply, develop and retain personnel, is an element within the budget itself. Thus, the manpower planning process provides an input to the budgeting process. In practice this will mean that the costing in the manpower planning programme will modify an assumed cost in the budget.

Because manpower planning both provides an input to the budget and is constrained by it, it is essential that financial and manpower planning be integrated. In particular, their timetables should correspond. When the most suitable means of reconciliation have been decided, the actions entailed form the manpower plan. As shown in Fig. 2.1, the manpower plan achieves a balance between demand and supply. In this way, the planning and control of manpower resources is incorporated into company planning, which is the first objective of the manpower planning programme.

The manpower plan has four major elements, as shown in Fig. 2.2.

Utilisation

Targets for improved productivity cannot be set until it is possible to measure productivity. When it is possible, management can set targets not only in the knowledge that it will be possible to monitor success in achieving them, but also with confidence in their practicability, for past trends and comparisons with other companies will together give an indication of what can be achieved.

FIG. 2.2   Manpower plan

Further, it will be necessary to consider in general terms how improvements are to be achieved. It is too easy to forecast an increased rate of improvement without considering the way of achieving this. The manpower plan must specify, at least in outline, where improvements are to be made and how.

The overall manpower targets for the first year of the forecast form what may be called 'the establishment'.

Manpower utilisation studies do not in themselves improve productivity. They do, however, provide the basis for management to plan improvements. The manpower planning process sets these plans in their context and enables management to monitor their results. This is relevant to all measures for achieving improvement, including negotiations about productivity. Management need to be able to assess what they need and what it is worth in such negotiations.

Supply

The recruitment programme necessary to supplement the internal manpower supply should be set out. Any expected problems in it, arising perhaps from difficult labour market conditions, should be considered and the steps necessary to overcome them planned.

Promotion policy involves changes in the supply of manpower available internally. It may be necessary to decide to alter past policy, possibly speeding up or slowing down the promotion rates. Naturally, if the rate is to be slowed down there could be attendant personnel problems, because staff will have their own expectations based on past observations.

Transfers between departments or divisions also affect the manpower supply situation. Policies designed to enhance the experience of staff by increasing mobility must be taken into account. On the other hand, the policies themselves should be made against the background of manpower demand.

Finally, if the situation of a future excess of manpower in any particular category is likely to arise and it cannot be solved by transfer arrangements, the redundancy programme can be planned well in advance.

Training

The development of staff, and the training schemes which form part of this development, should be planned on the basis of the future need for trained manpower. Both the supply and the utilisation plans have implications for training plans. The recruitment programme affects initial training schemes and plans for internal supply are the basis of continuation training. Promotion and transfer policies will also create training needs. Development plans may also be an element in the achievement of improved productivity.

Personnel policies

Most other aspects of personnel policy have a bearing on manpower supply, affecting both the ability to recruit and to retain staff. Remuneration and benefit policies and conditions of service are clearly relevant. Their major effect is probably on recruitment, but they may also affect retention. Decisions in these areas are not solely dependent on the manpower planning process: much other analytical work is required. Salary surveys and evaluation are necessary in order to know what action is necessary to maintain existing external and internal relativities. The manpower plan will indicate if these relativities must be changed or not.

Considerations of manpower demand and supply are relevant also to negotiations about pay and conditions. The fact that the company is known to think ahead about its manpower could well increase the unions' confidence in any statement of its intentions.

The retention of staff is dependent to a large extent on the atmosphere in which they work. This atmosphere is created for them by management and is, therefore, in some measure within management control. The manpower planning process can demonstrate the urgency or otherwise of changes in policies concerning these management/employee relations, so that costs involved can be sensibly evaluated.

These four elements of the manpower plan show how personnel policies are coordinated with each other and with the company's objectives, which is the second objective of a manpower planning programme.

There is a widespread idea that planning destroys individual initiative and freedom of choice and thus negates much of what personnel management stands for. This is the reverse of the truth. Predicting the behaviour of groups is quite different from controlling the actions of individuals. Indeed, the company shows its concern for the individual by thinking of the future manpower situation, rather than by letting him absorb the shocks of uncontrolled and unexpected change.

LONG- AND SHORT-RANGE MANPOWER PLANNING

In general, there are two determinants of the period of time which should be covered by manpower forecasts: the need for, and feasibility of, drawing up company plans for the period and the utility of the manpower plans. These two determinants are parallel to the two objectives of including manpower in company resource planning and of co-ordinating personnel policies. However, they can be in conflict. In a fast-changing marketing company the company planning period may be short, although at present it is almost invariably considerably longer than the time in fact allowed to the personnel department to organise a recruitment campaign. However, the training period required for a graduate entering the marketing department may be a year. Since the 'lead time' (the time required to recruit, train and instal in a fully effective job) must include the period from early in the year, when the university round of recruitment takes place, until he is fully trained any rational decision on recruitment policy requires a forecast of demand for trained marketing men at least eighteen months ahead.

Consider then the forecasting span required to decide on an apprentice intake, when their training takes five years in many cases and usually at least four. These specific problems are dealt with further in chapter 6, but they do indicate some of the difficulties involved in selecting the forecasting span.

A compromise may be the only solution. A detailed manpower plan can only be made for the period covered by the company's normal operational planning span, but a less detailed plan may be necessary for a subsequent period. If necessary, this must be based on a rough indication of where the company is going. This indication should be given by the Board or the Chief Executive. It is not part of the manpower planner's duty to forecast what policies his superiors are going to adopt.

Even if the company's business plans do extend far enough ahead for manpower planning purposes, it is probable that the early period will be forecast in more detail than the later period. The first part, which may be for one or two years, can be called the Operational, or Short-range, Plan, and the second part, perhaps covering the next three to five years, the Long-range Plan. Manpower planning should be similarly divided. Since the basis of the manpower demand forecasts is the company's plan, this necessarily follows. But there are sound reasons within the manpower planning process for this also.

The line manager's concern is essentially with relatively short-term problems. He is therefore concerned with the work load and manning of his department in the near future, probably for the next year or so. It is likely too that he makes budget proposals for the subsequent year and is supplied by his superiors with knowledge of company objectives in sufficient detail to do this. If he is also to be controlled by this budget he will be all the more anxious to think ahead carefully. Once manpower planning is established, it will be integrated with the budgetary procedure. Therefore the line manager will be deeply involved in the short-range forecast.

The short-range forecasts would be fairly detailed and lead to the tactical plans for recruitment, specifying numbers, and for training, examining the detail of different types of training. Long-range plans are much more concerned with strategic problems, giving an indication of the overall direction of manpower policies and forecasting manpower in less detailed terms. As such, their use lies in their value to top management in deciding company policy, and the involvement of line management, who will not see the relevance to their problems, should be less. Because of this, it is recommended that the two parts of manpower planning should be given a different emphasis. The forecasts for the short-range plan should be primarily the responsibility of line management, whereas the responsibility for the long-range forecasts should lie with the manpower planning unit.

However, the unit will require advice based on the knowledge of line management in making its long-range forecasts. One way to do this is for the manpower planning unit to do its analytical work and then translate the company's objectives into a forecast. On the basis of this they can discuss the forecast with line management, so that their perception of the situation can be incorporated in the final plan. With this basis it will be found that line managers can make a much more effective contribution than they could in the vacuum before any forecasts were made.

In the case of the short-range forecast, however, the emphasis is the other way round. The line manager should make his own forecast, because he is so intimately concerned with it, but he will need the backing of the systematic analysis of manpower. This is the task of the manpower planner. In the smaller organisation, this work may be done by the same unit (which may be only one man) which makes the long-range forecast. In the larger organisation, line management may rely on its own support staff.

The two types of planning do, in fact, interact with each other. Eventually, the long-range forecast will provide the background against which the short-range forecasts are made. This does not imply, of course, that the short-range forecast must be made to agree with the long-range. Forecasting is a dynamic process and circumstances do not remain constant. However, longer term considerations could affect decisions incorporated in the short-term plan.

Initially the data required for an acceptable degree of accuracy in long-range planning may not be available. The short-range process will begin to generate some of it and thus make long-range forecasting possible. Some will be collected in the analytical stage before forecasts are made, but these are data already available. A more important source will be the monitoring reports from the short-range exercise.

Monitoring is an essential part of the planning process and serves three purposes in addition to building up data for future use. First, it serves as a feedback mechanism for management, allowing management to react as soon as possible to a changed, unplanned situation. Secondly, it is a feedback to the manpower planner, enabling him to assess the validity of his techniques, especially if the situation is unchanged. Thirdly, it provides the means of control over the use of manpower to management, by constantly giving information and comparing it with the approved plan.

The distinction between long- and short-range planning, in both general, corporate planning and manpower planning itself, is not necessarily as distinct as this dichotomy of long-range and short-range suggests. Rather there is a continuum along which the emphasis changes from the philosophy and procedures appropriate to one, to those appropriate to the other. The distinction is made to bring out the conceptual differences between the two ends of the continuum.

Furthermore, what was the third year will, in due course, become the second year, so that the two types change from one to the other. Naturally, the interaction of the two types of manpower planning is also mirrored in the interaction of long- and short-term corporate planning. Decisions about the next year can vary according to a choice of goals in the longer term future: similarly, short-term changes—for example, in the market situation of the company—can affect the plans for the fourth or fifth year.

This process has been termed 'rolling planning and review'. In the context of the marketing programme, E. F. L. Brech [1] has described it thus:

Suppose the managing director is taking a *four-year forward look*. He frames his thinking in terms of a rolling cycle, with an inbuilt flexibility, the later years to be re-adjusted in the light of the actual performances and experiences of the earlier ones. The fourth-year targets will be broad-based objectives as to product-range and scale of turnover, with main financial requirements and expected profits. . . . The managing director has been able to fill in the *third year* more fully. Some of the assumptions can be firmer because, perhaps, they stem from what is firmly expected to happen in the second year. . . . The *second and first years* are little other than an extension of normal budgeting. Because planning is of the essence of management, the team of senior managers will have collaborated with the managing director in the formulation of the programme and budget for these years immediately coming, i.e. the first and second years of the rolling cycle.

This shows the same emphases in the different stages—for example, the involvement of other managers particularly in the shorter term plans—in the marketing plan as in the manpower plan. This is not surprising, for the manpower plan ought to derive from the marketing plan and feed back into it. Indeed, the manpower plan cannot exist without some form of corporate plan and the corporate plan must be supported by some form of plan concerning the resource of manpower, although too often this manpower plan will just be in the form of an unsupported assumption, perhaps not even explicit, that manpower requirements of the plan will be automatically forthcoming without any major problems.

In organisational terms, therefore, the manpower plan may derive from and feed back into the corporate plan of the company, but it is in reality an inseparable part of the company's total plan. The subsequent chapters, however, concentrate on the manpower 'part' of the total planning process, examine the techniques which might be involved in it and the organisation required to make them work.

3

Manpower demand forecasts

There are two major inputs to the manpower planning process, both for long-term and short-term planning: the demand forecast and the internal supply forecast. Nor does the forecasting method adopted necessarily depend on whether the planning is for the long or short term. The circumstances in which the forecast is made are more important, although the short-term forecast is likely to be less complex in its methodology, and more detailed in its content.

The circumstances in which the forecast is made include the planning methods adopted in the company, the methods possible in relation to the type and mix of products, the type and mix of manpower and the data available. It is important to realise how significant this last factor is. To try out a forecasting method, the manpower planner is likely to want data over a period of time. Therefore, to get quick results data must extend some way into the past. But more than that, they must be accessible, so that he can use them without undue searching and collating, and also be intelligible and consistent. The fact that data are available now will not help if past records have not been retained, nor will it help if the basis for collection has changed in some unremembered way.

It may frequently be that the forecasting methods are restricted by the availability of data or that insufficient data is available to demonstrate fully the soundness of the method which seems intuitively right. Obviously, the next step is to set up systems which will build up the store of data required for the future. However, even if the existing data are poor, it is suggested that a start should be made on some rudimentary manpower planning.

The main reason for this suggestion is that manpower decisions will be made in any case and even rudimentary planning may improve the quality of those decisions. There are two further reasons. First, unless there is a clear need for the data, it may be impossible to sustain the systems for their collection or at least to ensure that there is any effort to ensure accuracy. Professor D. J. Bartholomew has written:

> Data is collected to satisfy some particular demand and hence until manpower planners specify what data they need, none will be available. The practical value of advanced model building is that it creates a blue-print for the kind of data which is necessary for effective manpower planning [1].

Secondly, the nature of the data requirements may not be fully realised until the process of using them has begun.

The analysis of data provides a relationship between manpower and output or work load, and this chapter sets out the main ways in which this relationship can be established. The relationship can then be used to forecast manpower demand in the future on the assumption of a given output level or several possible levels.

It follows from this that the manpower planner must have a detailed knowledge of company's plans for future output. It has already been argued that manpower planning is a part of the total plan of the company and the link is very clear at this stage of forming forecasts as well as in the integration of decisions stemming from the various forecasts. If manpower planning is held to be a personnel function (and this is discussed further in chapter 10), the company must ensure the inclusion of the function in the management decision-making process. In spite of the importance of the resource of manpower, managements frequently do not involve personnel managers in their decisions. Indeed, a survey has shown that personnel managers are often not informed of decisions, let alone involved in them [2].

There are two main factors to be assessed in the analyses for demand forecasting. First, the volume of output will clearly have an effect on manpower, occasionally in a quite simple, direct way, but more often there will be a complication. Secondly, the level of productivity affects this relationship between manpower and output. These factors are interrelated, but we shall first examine them independently. They are, in fact, two dimensions of the same problem. The former is an analysis of the change in manpower demand occasioned by changing the output in volume or mix: this is here called *analysis of performance*. The latter is an analysis of the change in manpower occasioned by changing productivity, which alters over time, and is here called *analysis of productivity*.

ANALYSIS OF PERFORMANCE

In order to derive the manpower demand forecast from the business plan, the relationship between work load and manpower requirements must be estimated. A number of methods can be considered, but it is not possible to specify which is the most suitable. Apart from the constraints imposed by data availability and the circumstances of the organisation, there is the problem that demand forecasting at the level of the firm has been researched much less than internal supply forecasting.

In making the forecast, it is necessary normally to divide the manpower in certain categories.[1] If a detailed manpower category system is being used it will probably be necessary to group these together for most forecasting methods. Two courses are then open to the manpower planner.

First, he may analyse the performance of different categories of manpower separately. For example, he may measure the number of craftsmen needed for a particular level of output and use this to make a forecast of craftsmen, and then separately analyse the number of semiskilled workers needed for this same level and thus predict their numbers.

Second, he may analyse the total numbers of the manpower used and predict from this analysis, subsequently dividing into the different categories of manpower. This may be done by assuming the continuance of the same proportions or by analysing the trend of these changing proportions. (The same methods are available for analysing the relationship between different categories of manpower as for analysing the relationship between manpower and work load.)

Either of the methods, separate analysis for different categories or subsequent proportional division, can be tested by analysing the data of these relationships in the past.

Fundamentally, all methods of analysis of performance derive from an analysis of the past, but they can be classified into three groups: direct analysis, standard relationships, and the inductive method. They all depend on the validity of the assumption that developments in the future will exhibit some continuity with the past.

[1] See chapter 8 on manpower categories.

Direct analysis: ratios and regression

The simplest method of analysis of past performance is to derive a *ratio* between two variables (work load and manpower of a certain category). This can be derived from the figures relating to a particular point in time or from figures averaged over a period of time.

The ratio demonstrates very clearly the two aspects of forecasting—analysis of performance and of productivity, as two simple examples will show:

Example A

Company 1	Company 2
$£x$ of sales requires 10 salesmen	$£x$ of sales requires 10 salesmen
$£2x$ of sales requires 20 salesmen	$£2x$ of sales requires 15 salesmen

Example B

Company 3	Company 4
$£x$ of sales last year required 10 salesmen	$£x$ of sales last year required 10 salesmen
$£x$ of sales this year requires 10 salesmen	$£x$ of sales this year requires 8 salesmen

In example *A*, Company 1 has a constant ratio: the doubling of sales requires a doubling of the sales force. Company 2, on the other hand, can double its sales with the addition of only five salesmen: it is achieving an economy of scale. (One can find the opposite situation if there is a degree of market saturation: it may be that any increment to existing sales requires a disproportionately large effort.)

In example *B*, Company 3 has a constant ratio again, but this is constant over time, whereas Company 4 has improved its ratio over time: it has increased its productivity.

The changing ratio can be dealt with by *linear regression* and we are concerned at the moment to apply such a method to analyse performance, i.e. to examine the problem of Company 2 in example *A*. The description of techniques here and throughout the book is intended to give an understanding of what they can achieve: for a more detailed treatment of most statistical techniques which are of use in manpower planning, yet nevertheless a treatment which is intelligible to the non-statistician, the reader is referred to K. A. Yeomans [3].

Figure 3.1 shows how the relationship between a number of 'observations' of the relationship of two variables—in this case, manpower and razor blades produced—can be plotted on a graph. The relationship between the two variables is indicated by the line drawn on the graph. This line can, of course, be drawn by eye and this may well give a sufficiently accurate result. Linear regression is, however, the statistical technique for establishing this 'line of best fit'.

Clearly, one cannot draw any line until one has two observations and even two observations are really totally insufficient. Regression analysis not only specifies the line of best fit, but also provides a measure of its accuracy. It provides a correlation coefficient, which indicates the

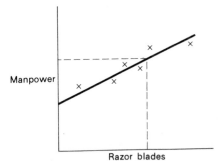

FIG. 3.1   Regression analysis

degree of linear association between the two variables, a coefficient of 0 indicating no association and of 1 indicating complete or 'perfect' association. In addition, the calculation will show how probable it is that one could get the coefficient by chance. Thus, if the calculation shows the correlation to be 0·9, which indicates a high degree of linear association, it will also be possible to calculate that one can be, say, 95 per cent certain that this result is not achieved by chance. The larger the number of observations, the higher the degree of certainty which can be obtained, and until there are three observations one can get no measure at all of correlation or of certainty. It is worth remembering in this context that, if analysis is being based on annual production and annual average manpower, the number of observations can be doubled by taking six-monthly figures instead, though the data may not allow this.

It must also be emphasised that a basic assumption is being made—that the relationship is linear. It could well be that one should not be trying to fit a straight line to the data in Fig. 3.1, but some sort of curve. If a straight line provides a good fit, naturally it justifies using the technique. If, on the other hand, the correlation is low it does not prove that there is no association between the variables, but that the association, if there is one, is not linear.

Thus regression analysis seeks to provide a measure of the extent to which movements in the values of the two variables are correlated with each other. The aim is then to predict changes in one variable (the dependent variable) by reference to changes in the other (the independent or explanatory variable), where the future values of this independent variable are already postulated.

Thus in the example in Fig. 3.1, if there is found to be a high correlation between manpower and razor blades produced, then it is possible to predict the manpower requirement for a planned level of production, by reading the figure off the graph (as shown by the dotted line) or by inserting the production figure in the formula which will have been calculated.

The relationship between the variables is in the linear form:

$$y = a + bx$$

where a and b are constants. This equation expresses the regression of the dependent variable y (in this case, manpower) on the independent variable x (production of razor blades). Once the line of best fit has been established, it is possible to predict changes in y (manpower) by reference to changes in x (production). Thus, for example, the regression analysis might give a formula:

$$y = 70 + 0.1x$$

where y = manpower and x = blades produced in millions.

If planned production was 800 million blades in a year, the calculation would be:

$$y = 70 + 0.1 \times 800$$
$$= 70 + 80$$
$$= 150 \text{ men}$$

It is important to distinguish the dependent variable (in this case, manpower) from the independent (in this case, blade production), because the regression analysis minimises the error in the dependent variable. A different linear relationship would be given if the blade production was to be calculated from the manpower, in which case the error in the dependent variable (now blade production) would be minimised. By tradition, the dependent variable is called y and the independent variable x, and the whole regression is called a regression of 'y given x' or $y(x)$.

Predictions should be made within the range of the experimental data if this is at all possible. Extrapolation beyond this range has very doubtful validity. Thus if in the past production had always varied between 200 and 500 million blades it would be unwise to place much faith in the formula derived from these data as a means of forecasting manpower needed to produce a 1,000 million blades.

Manpower is not necessarily dependent on only one other variable, but possibly on the combined effect of two or more. For example, the number of production staff may not be dependent merely on the number of blades produced, but also on the mix of production, i.e. the numbers of different types of blades produced.

Fundamentally, the approach adopted and the principles involved are exactly the same as for two-variable regression and correlation analysis. *Multiple regression analysis* allows manpower to be estimated from a number of independent variables, such as the number of carbon steel and of stainless steel razor blades.

Figure 3.2 shows this example in diagrammatic form. Now that we have three variables, instead of the two-dimensional graph of Fig. 3.1, we have a three-dimensional graph; and, instead of fitting a straight line, we are fitting a plane.

The multiple regression model for three variables gives a formula in the following form:

$$y_1 = a + bx_2 + cx_3$$

where y_1 is the dependent variable (manpower)

x_2 and x_3 are the independent variables (carbon blades and stainless blades)

a, b and c are constants.

It is possible to have more than three variables. Although the formula can then be calculated, it is impossible to represent the situation pictorially, because it would be necessary to have four or more dimensions.

Although any number of variables is possible, the higher the number of variables the greater the number of observations necessary. Just as two points are needed to fix a straight line and three even to begin to measure the correlation, so three points are needed to fix a plane and

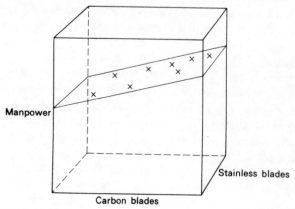

FIG. 3.2　Multiple regression analysis

four to begin to measure the correlation. Thus, if five variables are used, six observations are necessary to make any sense of the situation at all and, in fact, many more are needed usually to obtain a really reliable forecast. It is better normally to use only the most important variables: in real life, there will always be an unexplained variation and the omission of some of the less important variables will probably only add slightly to it. Once again, it must be emphasised that a fundamental assumption is being made—that it is a plane which should be fitted to the data represented in Fig. 3.2 and not a curved surface.

Linear regressions with two variables only are not difficult to calculate manually, especially with the aid of a desk calculator with an automatic square root. The method is given by Yeomans [3]. Multiple regressions are more difficult. However, the manual calculation does tend to discourage experimentation with different variables. Computer programs for regression analysis are readily available, usually in some standard statistical suite of programs, and the calculation then becomes a very simple operation.

Indirect analysis: standard relationships

An alternative approach is to base forecasts on some form of standard relationship between manpower and production. Such a relationship is derived from past data, but not necessarily the data of the operating unit concerned. Work study techniques can build up a manning standard or this standard may be arrived at by less rigorous methods. Predetermined motion timings (PMTs) can be used also in building up the standard. (Work study is a subject complete in itself: see, for example, R. M. Currie [4].)

In common with other forecasting methods, the starting point in the work-study-based approach is usually the sales or production plan for the appropriate planning period. In order to determine the manpower that will be needed, these forecasts have first to be converted to a production schedule (taking into account existing levels of stock). The production schedule is then split up into a programme of work for each main period (e.g. each year) with perhaps a more detailed programme (e.g. monthly) for the first main period.

This approach is particularly suitable for production line work. The maximum output of a production line is known. Plans may be made to introduce new production lines with known outputs and known manning standards (whether based on work study or not). It does depend, however, on knowing the manning standards and thus may be suitable only for relatively short-range plans; whereas a more generalised method, like regression analysis, may be necessary for longer-term forecasts, so that trends in manning standards can be incorporated.

The period over which such forecasts can be made does depend on the industry. The method is suitable for the Central Electricity Generating Board, for example, for the bulk of its staff, who are employed in the power stations. It takes at least five years, including the obtaining of planning permission, to build a power station. Closures of obsolete plant need much less planning time, but nevertheless can be planned tentatively some way ahead. After all, the decisions to build power stations are based on forecasts of the total demand for electricity and the closure of other stations is relevant to them. Staffing standards for planned stations are capable of being established fairly early; for the design of the station is necessarily decided upon early in the planning period. Thus, manpower planning becomes a basically simple matter of addition (for new stations) and subtraction (for closures). However, the problem of improving productivity standards remains. Although significant improvements in overall productivity result from the replacement of old plant by new and are thus, as it were, 'built-in' to the forecast, improvement in productivity through greater staff flexibility and changes in organisation have been particularly significant for these trends. (Productivity trends are examined below.)

An example which is almost exactly parallel is the Royal Navy, ships being very similar to power stations for manpower planning purposes, and their planning system has been described by A. R. Smith [5].

Indirect analysis: inductive method

Managers' own estimates of requirements also derive from their experience of the past, albeit in a less systematic but possibly more comprehensive way than other methods. Their estimates should also be taken into account alongside other methods of forecasting; because the future demand depends, sometimes to a large extent, on their intentions. This is particularly true of short-range forecasts, covering a period to which the manager is likely to have given considerable thought. In the longer term, managers' estimates are likely to be less helpful and it has already been suggested that some other method should be used to provide the background for discussion with managers.

In some cases, future numbers depend on numbers generated elsewhere in the forecasting process. For example, the number of training staff turns on the training requirement, and the training plan is at least partially dependent on the manpower planning process. It may be necessary to make an estimate, because of systems within the company which make it necessary to provide figures. In this case assumptions must be clearly stated so that subsequent modifications can, if necessary, easily be made.

There are other cases of interdependence of forecasts. For example, the manpower in some support functions, like plant maintenance, may be found to correlate more highly with production manpower than other measures for which data is available. Thus, the production manpower forecast gives rise to the plant maintenance forecast. However, whereas training manpower is dependent on decisions at the planning stage, which is a later stage in the planning cycle, the plant maintenance forecast is derived directly from a demand forecast, and is not likely, therefore, to cause problems of delay.

ANALYSIS OF PRODUCTIVITY

Productivity is the relationship between volume of production and manpower used, but the variety of measures available for each term is such that this is by no means an exact definition. It differs from performance in that it is dynamic—it changes over time and not over volume of production. Furthermore, it has two main components, technological change and manpower utilisation. The power station example has already distinguished the two. Technological change, which at one further remove could be called 'greater capital investment', often leads automatically to improved productivity. But this is not really what is being talked about when productivity bargains are being negotiated, although the two are often confused. The other aspect, manpower utilisation, is what is in the hands of the trade unions and of the ordinary line manager. Better management, better organisation and better worker cooperation can all lead to improved productivity in isolation from or together with technological change.

The power station example also shows the importance of distinguishing the two components; for, in the standard relationship method, technological change is built into the forecast, whereas manpower utilisation is not, and in the direct analysis method neither component is included.

The improvement of productivity is important in its own right. But it cannot be pursued in isolation from the examination of other plans for manpower and the other resources. Technological change usually depends on capital investment: better cooperation may entail remuneration changes, creating an additional revenue cost. The manpower planning process creates a mechanism by which productivity plans can be considered in relation to other plans, so that, as far as possible, the aim of the best possible conjunction of resources is achieved. This is one way in which productivity and manpower planning are interconnected.

The manpower planning process itself, however, requires analyses of productivity, in order that manpower demand forecasts can be made. First, it is important to eliminate as quickly as possible any existing misutilisations of manpower; otherwise, they become incorporated in the base of the forecast and there is thus the danger that they will be perpetuated. Indeed, in an expanding situation, they might be magnified. Secondly, future improvements must be forecast. It is usually necessary to make some separate assessment of one or both of the components of productivity. For example, the methods of analysing performance given above all require some modification.

The ratio method is very easily modified for changes over time. A *ratio time series* can be plotted in a graph as in Fig. 3.3. Thus the change in the ratio over time can be examined and future changes can be predicted. If the change seems to be linear, i.e. if observations fall roughly in a straight line, linear regression can be used to obtain the line of best fit, just as it was used to predict the change in the relationship of manpower to production above.

The regression methods of analysing performance assume a constant level of marginal productivity, and forecasts made in this way thus assume the projection into the future of this level. What this means can best be explained graphically. Figure 3.4 shows a simple graph of manpower and output. The line OA shows a possible relationship between the two: for 10 units of production 10 men are required, for 20 units 20 men and so on, so that the productivity ratio is always 1. Line OB shows a different relationship: for 10 units of production 5 men are needed, for 20 units 10 men and so on, the productivity ratio being 0·5. Thus, linear relationships of this sort represent a constant level of productivity.

In this example, however, the lines shown go through the origin of

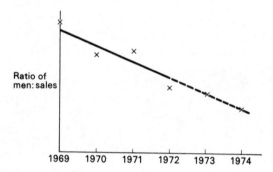

FIG. 3.3   Ratio time series

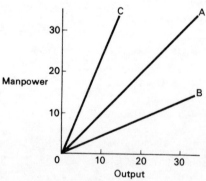

FIG. 3.4   Constant productivity

the graph. In Fig. 3.5 they do not; and the lines on this graph represent the equations normally found as a result of regression analysis. As has been said, the equation is of the form:

$$y = a + bx$$

where a and b are constants.

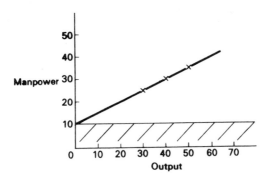

FIG. 3.5   Constant marginal productivity

In this equation, b gives the slope of the line and a gives the point at which the line cuts the vertical or y axis of the graph. In Fig. 3.5 the line cuts the y axis at 10 men. The rationale of this presumably would be that one needs 10 men even if there is no production. In fact, however, the points plotted are all well away from the y axis and show that for 30 units of production 25 men are required, for 40 units 30 men, for 50 units 35 men and so on. The productivity ratios are thus:

Production units	Manpower	Productivity ratio
30	25	0·83
40	30	0·75
50	35	0.7

The productivity is changing as production goes up. However, the marginal rate, i.e. ignoring the ten men required anyway who are represented by the shaded block on the graph, will be found to be 0·5, thus:

Production units	Manpower	Marginal productivity
30	10+15	$\frac{15}{30}=0\cdot5$
40	10+20	$\frac{20}{40}=0\cdot5$
50	10+25	$\frac{25}{50}=0\cdot5$

The equation for this particular example is:

$$y=10+0\cdot5x$$

where y is the manpower required and x the production units. It is necessary to understand this concept of marginal productivity, so that modifications to the forecast can be made.

Standard relationship methods, as has already been pointed out, normally incorporate the technological element of productivity, but not the utilisation part, so that there is a need for a separate analysis to enable modifications to be made.

In the inductive method, managers would incorporate an assessment of future changes, but it is useful nevertheless to have a guide to levels and changes in the past, so that the manpower planner has some factual background against which to discuss the managers' forecasts.

In order to forecast productivity it is necessary to measure it. Several methods have been used, but in the main they are refinements to the ratio of manpower to output. Productivity changes over time and the change in the ratio over time is, in fact, the ratio time series. As has been indicated, this can be used by itself for forecasting manpower demand. It may also be used as the background to modifications of demand forecasts made by other methods.

Productivity is a much more complex concept than this ratio. The ratio is a measure of one aspect only: it is a 'partial' index. An index which measures the output of refined oil, for example, in terms of barrels per man employed not only ignores other relevant factors, like the degrees of capital intensiveness, but also takes no account of what categories of manpower are included and what they cost. It may be sensible in Britain to use more manpower and less capital equipment than in the USA, where manpower costs more. Nevertheless, if less manpower is used in the USA, this fact demonstrates that it is possible to use less manpower (although it may not be desirable).

For the manpower planner, such an index does show the changes over time and provide a basis on which to forecast changes in productivity. It is this partial index which he requires, rather than a more complex measure; for he is concerned with forecasting the change in the relationship of manpower to output. If the partial nature of indices is clearly understood, even relatively crude measures can provide useful indicators of future possibilities. If any such indicators are available, they should be used as background.

Whether or not such indices are available, forecasts of manpower demand, whatever their method of production, should be separately assessed by management with a view to incorporating productivity improvements. Even if the forecast is itself inductive, it is helpful to consider productivity separately. This assessment is necessary if only because many improvements depend on management's future actions, which might currently be intentions, and hence capable of being formulated. The assessment requires consideration of:

- Any indicators of productivity trends.
- The distinction between improved utilisation and technological change and, consequently, a knowledge of planned and likely advances in technology.
- The extent to which improvements resulting from either better utilisation or technological change are already incorporated in the forecast, which is dependent on the forecasting method used.
- Planned or likely changes in organizational structure and methods, which frequently have an effect on productivity.

It is useful to set out a list of factors which will affect productivity and consider each one separately. If the numbers being dealt with are quite large the effect of each factor can be quantified and an overall factor worked out. This method is based on one described by I. G. Helps at a Conference organised by the Manpower Planning Study Group [6].

	Improvement in 3 years (%)	Factor giving change in manpower in 3 years	
New organisation structure	6	0·94	This gives
Better equipment	5	0·95	a combined
New information requirements (i.e. increased effort involved)	−8	1·08	effect on manpower
Greater staff flexibility (achieved through negotiation)	10	0·90	productivity
Training	8	0·92	of 0·80

The factor in the last column is the proportion of manpower remaining after the improvement has been made, i.e.

	Improvement	*Factor*
New organisation structure	6% or 0·06	1·00−0·06 = 0·94

The combined total effect is arrived at by multiplying the individual factors, i.e.:

$$0·94 \times 0·95 \times 1·08 \times 0·90 \times 0·92 = 0·80$$

It is possible to use this method not only for dealing with productivity changes but also with changes in manpower demand. It is also possible to extend the method to include a fairly arbitrary measure of probability, but this refinement is likely only to be practical if large numbers are involved. Managers are required to give a most likely, a pessimistic and an optimistic forecast, and they may not find this very easy to do in practice. (See note at end of this chapter for the refinement.)

COMBINING PERFORMANCE AND PRODUCTIVITY

In examining performance and productivity, we have assumed that they could be analysed separately and that they would be combined in some more or less subjective way. When we analyse past data, however, the two elements are normally inextricably mixed. They can be separated only if the volume of output has been constant over the period for which data are being examined. In such a case, any changes in manpower are due to productivity changes. If manpower is unchanged as well as output, productivity is unchanged also. Normally, however, volume of output varies. Productivity, which varies over time, can also be assumed to be changing.

Some progress can be made in understanding this situation on the basis of two hypotheses:

1. That increased output affects manpower according to a linear relationship. We have already seen that increased production may require a disproportionately smaller increase in manpower and, although in some fairly exceptional circumstances a disproportionately higher number of men may be required, we shall call this effect *economy of scale*.

2. That productivity increases over time and that this relationship between output and manpower follows a *learning curve*.

The learning curve, if applied to individuals, shows the rate at which they learn. As one might expect, the tendency is for the rate to improve fairly rapidly at first and then to slacken gradually until the peak performance is reached. Figure 3.6 shows the form of the curve. It has been shown, notably in relation to aircraft production in World War II, that this same principle is applicable to organisations undertaking the same task [7, 8]. The curve is usually drawn as the falling relationship between the man-hours per unit of output and the cumulative output, i.e. the falling manpower requirement as time progresses. This is shown in Fig. 3.7. The curve follows what is called the 'doubled output unit rule'. This is demonstrated in the following table:

TABLE 3.1   Doubled output unit rule

1st unit requires 200 man-hours
2nd unit requires $x\%$ less hours than 1st unit
4th unit requires $x\%$ less hours than 2nd unit
8th unit requires $x\%$ less hours than 4th unit
16th unit requires $x\%$ less hours than 8th unit
   and so on, where x is constant.

Returning to our two hypotheses, we can separate the two elements, economy of scale and learning curve, theoretically, even if it is impossible in a real-life analysis of data. Economy of scale depends on two variables, the rate of growth in scale and the relationship (assumed to be linear) which growth bears to manpower. In the one extreme case, if there is no growth, there will be no economy of scale. In the other extreme, there can be growth but no economy of scale, if each successive increment to production requires additional manpower according to the same ratio as the original output per man.

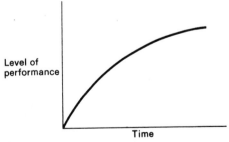

FIG. 3.6   Learning curve

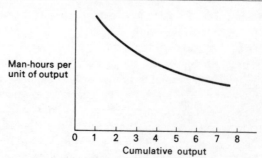

FIG. 3.7 Learning curve—doubled output unit rule

Figure 3.8 shows this graphically. Output is plotted against manpower, as in the examples of regression analysis already discussed. It is assumed that there is no 'learning curve effect'. The one extreme, where there is no growth and hence no change in manpower is represented by a single point on such a graph. For example, 100 units of production require 100 men at point A. The other extreme of growth without economy of scale is shown by the line AB, on which 100 units require 100 men and 150 units 150 men.

If, however, there is economy of scale and it is in accordance with a constant level of 'marginal productivity', a line such as AC will be produced. This shows manpower growing at only 50 per cent of the increment to production (which we have called 50 per cent economy of scale). Line AD shows a 75 per cent economy of scale line, i.e. extra

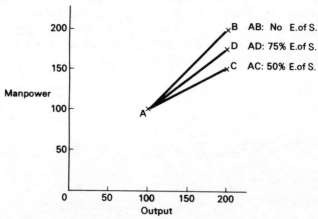

FIG. 3.8 Economy of scale

manpower required is 75 per cent of each increment to production. It can be seen that this is the same principle as that shown in Fig. 3.5. When actual data is plotted on a graph such as this it can be called a *scatter plot*.

Let us turn to the learning curve effect. This might show that the first 100 units of production would use 100 men and that the second 100 units used a certain percentage less. For example, the second 100 units might use 10 per cent less, i.e. 90 men. We could call this a 10 per cent learning curve. It becomes immediately obvious that we cannot plot this on a scatter plot like Fig. 3.8. Manpower must be plotted against cumulative production. Figure 3.9 shows a 10 per cent

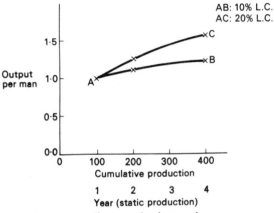

FIG. 3.9   Learning curve effect—ratio time series

(AB) and a 20 per cent (AC) learning curve plotted as a productivity ratio against cumulative production.

If there was a static level of production of 100 units per year, each 100 units on the cumulative output scale would represent the year and this is shown on the graph also. The curves are, therefore, marked 'static production', and the graph becomes a *ratio time series*. If production were, in fact, growing, this fact would affect the curves on a ratio time series: Fig. 3.10 reproduces the 10 per cent learning curve and the 20 per cent learning curve with static production (AB and AC) and this is the same as in Fig. 3.9. It also shows the 20 per cent learning curve with a 20 per cent per annum growth rate (AD), showing how the growth makes the curve steeper, since the doubled production point is reached earlier.

With these concepts as background it is necessary to consider what the combined effect of economy of scale and the learning curve might be when manpower and production data are plotted on either a scatter plot or a ratio time series. A number of possible combinations are shown in Figs 3.11 and 3.12. Figure 3.11 is a scatter plot and shows two of the same economy of scale lines as Fig. 3.8. It also shows some curves which incorporate the learning curve effect, which can be shown on a scatter plot once a particular rate of growth has been assumed. (If output were constant, manpower would decrease with learning nevertheless, giving a vertical, and thus unintelligible, line on the graph.) It will be noted that the learning curve effect reduces until the curves

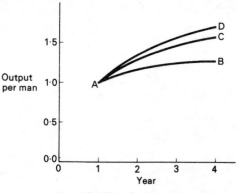

Line AB: 10% L.C. with static production
Line AC: 20% L.C. with static production
Line AD: 20% L.C. with 20% p.a. increase in growth rate

FIG. 3.10   Learning curve and growth: ratio time series

approximate closely to straight lines, thus justifying a linear regression analysis if the initial learning stage is past. (Table 3.2 gives the calculations for the curves shown.)

Figure 3.12 is a ratio time series and shows curves based on the same data as were used in Fig. 3.11. Note that line AC, which is affected by economy of scale alone, curves one way, whilst line AD, which is affected by learning curve effects, curves the other. In line AE these effects almost balance each other out and the line is almost straight. The 100 per cent economy of scale line, AB in Fig. 3.11, would be represented by the horizontal axis on a ratio time series like this one.

These two figures provide the background to the interpretation of actual data plotted in these two ways. Naturally, if rates of growth vary

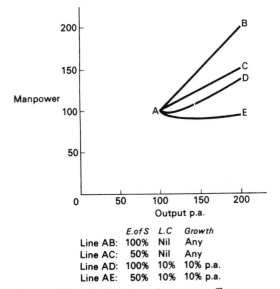

	E.of S	L.C	Growth
Line AB:	100%	Nil	Any
Line AC:	50%	Nil	Any
Line AD:	100%	10%	10% p.a.
Line AE:	50%	10%	10% p.a.

FIG. 3.11   Scatter plot, showing learning curve effect

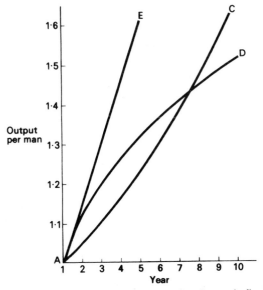

(The lines show the same situations as in figure 3.11)

FIG. 3.12   Ratio time series, showing economy of scale effect

TABLE 3.2   Calculations for Figs. 3.11 and 3.12

Year	Output: 10% p.a. growth	Cumulative output	10% LC ratio	100% E of S ratio	Combined ratio	Man-power
Line AD						
1	100	100	1·0	1·0	1·0	100
2	110	210	1·12	1·0	1·12	98
3	121	331	1·19	1·0	1·19	102
4	133	464	1·26	1·0	1·26	106
5	146	610	1·32	1·0	1·32	111
6	161	771	1·37	1·0	1·37	117
7	177	948	1·41	1·0	1·41	125
8	195	1143	1·45	1·0	1·45	135
9	214	1357	1·49	1·0	1·49	144
10	235	1592	1·52	1·0	1·52	155
Line AE				50% E of S ratio		
1	100	100	1·0	1·0	1·0	100
2	110	210	1·12	1·05	1·18	93
3	121	331	1·19	1·11	1·32	92
4	133	464	1·26	1·17	1·47	91
5	146	610	1·32	1·23	1·62	90
6	161	771	1·37	1·31	1·79	90
7	177	948	1·41	1·39	1·96	90
8	195	1143	1·45	1·48	2·14	91
9	214	1357	1·49	1·57	2·34	92
10	235	1592	1·52	1·66	2·52	93

Note: The learning curve ratios can be read from a graph such as Fig. 3.9.

the curves are distorted, and it is necessary to experiment with the actual data to begin to understand the patterns of change involved. At present no more exact method of interpretation can be offered. Indeed, whether or not this degree of sophistication is required will depend on the availability of data, the apparent reliability of the less complex interpretation, like the use of regression analysis without these modifications, and also the expectations and understanding of the top management of the organisation. The forecasts are made as a basis for their decision-making. They must, therefore, be able to interpret them, even though they do not need to understand exactly the detail of the forecasting methods involved.

NOTE ON PROBABILITY ELEMENT IN FORECASTING METHOD PROPOSED BY I.G. HELPS

Probability is assumed to have a beta distribution. Each estimate is given as three figures: most likely (m), pessimistic (p) and optimistic (r). Then,

$$\text{Mean value } (E) = \frac{p + 4m + r}{6} \tag{1}$$

$$\text{Standard deviation } (s) = \frac{r - p}{6} \tag{2}$$

It is necessary to translate deviations into absolute measures to combine them, so that the coefficient of variation is used:

$$\text{Coefficient of variation } (C) = \frac{s}{E} \tag{3}$$

This coefficient can be combined by adding the squared values. An example given by I. G. Helps was:

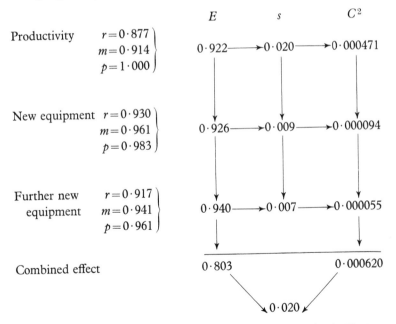

The arrows show the sequence of calculation. The combined effect on E is arrived at by multiplying the figures in column E: 0.922×0.926

$\times 0.940 = 0.803$. For each horizontal line s is calculated by formula (2) above, then C is calculated by formula (3) above and squared. The C^2 values are combined by addition. Then s can be calculated from C^2 and E: $s = C \times E$.

4

Internal manpower supply forecasting

Manpower demand is one aspect of manpower forecasting. The other aspect is the supply of manpower to fulfil the demand. The supply of manpower may be obtained by recruitment from external sources or from internal sources: the staff may be already employed. Internal manpower supply forecasting is therefore concerned primarily with the retention of staff. It is also concerned with forecasting how they will change in the future, for example, by promotion or transfer within the organisation.

Both these aspects of internal supply forecasting are based on some form of analysis of the past. The retention of staff is likely to be analysed in some way already by the personnel department, although it is probably viewed the other way round, as labour turnover or wastage. Internal movements—transfers and promotions—may be less readily analysed, but this is clearly important for all except the crudest forms of forecast. Occasionally, one may have a very static work force, where internal movements are insignificant. Craftsmen, for example, usually remain in their craft. Nevertheless, it may be necessary here to analyse transitions from apprentice to craftsmen and from craftsmen to supervisor.

ANALYSIS OF RETENTION

The method of measuring wastage of staff used by most companies is the annual labour turnover index or percentage wastage rate. This is calculated according to the so-called BIM formula and expresses wastage as a percentage of the staff in post and thus 'at risk' of leaving, i.e.

$$\text{Annual labour turnover} = \frac{\text{Leavers in year}}{\text{Average staff in post in year}} \times 100$$

This method has the very limited advantage that it is more or less universally used and thus interfirm comparisons can be made. However, its usefulness as a measure of labour turnover is so suspect that even this advantage is of doubtful value. For it has serious disadvantages for the personnel manager in his normal work as well as for the manpower planner. These disadvantages stem from the fact that it takes no account of the characteristics of the work force, but only of its size. In particular, the characteristic found empirically to have in normal circumstances the most significant effect—length of service—is disregarded.

This is important from the point of view of the personnel manager using the labour turnover index as a means of assessing morale. He cannot, in fact, distinguish between a situation, on the one hand, where every man in a department of 100 men has left and been replaced once (Index = 100 per cent) and, on the other hand, where 10 posts have each had 10 different occupants, but 90 posts are still held by men who have been with the company for years (Index = 100 per cent). Both situations may call for action, but certainly not the same action.

A good example of the dangers of misinterpretation of the labour turnover index, and of its failure to analyse the situation meaningfully, can be found in the analysis of wastage rates in the Central Electricity Generating Board in the period 1964–66. This was the time of the introduction of staff status for industrial staff in the electricity supply industry, and it was confidently expected that this would have a good effect on morale. It would thus have been expected that labour turnover rates would go down. But they did not: they went up. There can be very little doubt about the reason for this. At the same time as the status agreement, but unconnected with it, an agreement was made to shorten the working week and this entailed the recruitment of additional shift teams in many power stations. Thus, at the same time as the working conditions changed and an improved labour turnover was expected, there was an influx of new staff whose probability of leaving was high, which would lead one to expect an increase in labour turnover.

The first point about this is that the normal index could have been misinterpreted with serious consequences for the Board's conduct of its industrial relations. The second point is that, although it was not misinterpreted, it did not provide a proper analysis of the situation. It was impossible to tell what effect the status agreement had on the underlying, length-of-service-related wastage patterns. Some of the methods outlined below would have provided this analysis, but they presented data requirements which could not be met in so large an organisation at that time, which was before the CEGB computerised their personnel records.

The labour turnover index is also difficult to interpret in assessing the operational and financial implications of a particular leaving rate. For example, if there are initial training costs, it is important to know whether it is normal for trainees to remain long enough to recoup these costs. Two examples of leaving patterns of a group of entrants are shown in Fig. 4.1. In Fig. 4.1a many leave before they have had any opportunity to recoup training costs. Figure 4.1b presents a more satisfactory picture. Yet these differences would be masked if the single labour turnover index were used, because at any given time the groups would be combined with other leavers in different length of service groups.

The shortcomings of the index in manpower planning are equally significant. The trend of the labour turnover index is meaningless, because changes over time will probably be distorted or even over-shadowed by changes in the length of service distribution. An increase in short-service staff, as in the CEGB example, will increase the index,

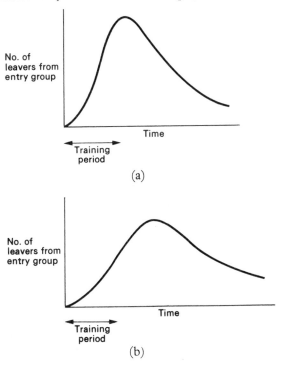

FIG. 4.1   Leaving patterns and training costs

but this does not indicate a continuing upward trend. Indeed, an increase may actually result from certain forecasts of manpower demand, and the supply forecast can only take proper account of this if it relates wastage to length of service. If an increase in staff is predicted, there will inevitably be many new (and, therefore, short-service) staff. The labour turnover index can be expected to go up if labour turnover characteristics remain the same: it will remain constant only if the characteristics change.

Similarly, if staff is to be reduced, one cannot predict a continuance of the existing labour turnover index. Once the short service staff have left and not been replaced, only longer service staff will remain. Their probability of leaving will be less and turnover will, in fact, decrease. The rate of contraction in numbers will thus be diminished. This can be crucial in planning a rundown of staff. It is easy to think that 'natural wastage' will take care of reductions, when the real situation is that natural wastage will reduce to a very low rate after recruitment has stopped.

Therefore, some method of measuring labour turnover which is service-specific is required.

Stability index

This is a fairly well-known measure and gives an index of the numbers who stayed throughout a period (e.g. a year) who could have stayed throughout it (i.e. were already employed at the beginning of it), e.g.

$$\frac{\text{Staff with 1 year's service at time } t}{\text{Staff in post at time } t-1} \times 100$$

It is complementary to the BIM labour turnover index, bringing out the truth in the 100 per cent turnover situation given above as an example. It is not suitable for forecasting because it does not distinguish the length of service of leavers and takes no account at all of staff who joined during the year (and who may also have left). Furthermore, it is not always easy to interpret what it means, even in conjunction with the labour turnover index, except in the most extreme cases. For example, an employee who joined the day before the period under analysis and an employee who joined ten years before, if they both left in the period, would be given equal weight in the index, although they possibly had two days' and nearly eleven years' service respectively.

Bowey's stability index

A rather different stability index, proposed by A. M. Bowey, should be mentioned. Like the stability index discussed above, it is for use in conjunction with a labour turnover index and is more concerned with the morale of the work force than with forecasting. It does, however, include everybody employed, unlike the previous stability index. It also takes properly into account varying lengths of service. The basis of this index is the expression of the total length of service of employees in service at the date of analysis as a percentage of the total possible length of service if the work force had experienced no labour turnover. In her first article on this [1] Angela Bowey talked of measuring this index over fifty years; more practically, in a subsequent article [2] she had adapted the method to a two-year period. (Other periods could be chosen.)

In this case, one takes the length of service in months of staff with less than two years' service and twenty-four months for each employee with two years' service or more. This total is expressed as a percentage of the length of service of a full staff complement over two years. If the work force varied in size over the period, this must be taken into account, thus:

$$\frac{L_n}{\sum_{i=1}^{x} n_i N_i} \times 100$$

where L_n = length of service of all employees with less than two years' service plus $24 \times$ number of employees with two years' service or more.

$\sum_{i=1}^{x} n_i N_i$ = sum of steps in expansion of labour force, at each step the size, N_i, being multiplied by the months it remained at this size, n_i.

This is shown graphically at Fig. 4.2. The index expresses as a figure the area under the curve as a proportion of the total possible area. Whilst different curves can give the same index, it is clear that they cannot be greatly different.

Cohort analysis

One proven method of analysing the retention of staff is cohort analysis. A group of staff who are as far as possible homogeneous and who joined the organisation at the same time (or within a given period of time) is followed over a period of time and the rate at which it wastes away is analysed. This group is known as a *cohort* (the word, in fact, means a tenth part of a Roman legion). The graphical representation of this analysis is known as a *log-normal wastage curve*, or if plotted as its converse, as a *survival curve*.

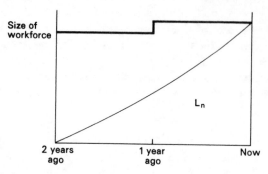

FIG. 4.2   Labour stability curve

The statistical theory behind this method was developed by Lane and Andrew [3] and it has been shown to be effective in a number of organisations. Its advantage is that, as is explained below, it is possible by means of a particular graphical presentation to express the curve, which is a log-normal curve, as a straight line.

A straight line is defined by two points, so that a prediction can easily be made. However, there are also disadvantages. First, the forecaster needs to have the first two points for each cohort to make his prediction; for cohorts vary one from another [4]. Yet he may need to forecast the wastage of groups who have not even joined the organisation, let alone begun to waste away. Secondly, if a full examination of wastage is to be made, each leaver must be related to his cohort and its size must be known. Since this could be a group who joined twenty years ago, the task usually presents insuperable problems of data collection. A third problem arises if the staff is relatively stable, as P. L. Ashdown [5] points out. The length of time over which a cohort must be followed can become quite great (with data collection problems attendant on this fact) and the consequent time lapse between the date of joining of the analysed cohort and of the forecasted cohort becomes so great that the validity of applying the data from one to the other is questionable. In effect, what is needed is a way of combining all the cohorts to give a single picture.

Nevertheless, the technique can be useful in analysing, and forecasting for, certain specific groups of staff, who have very similar characteristics and possibly who join at particular times of the year; for example, apprentice entrants and graduate recruits from university, although the CEGB report quoted above, did show the method to be applicable to a less cohesive group—the personnel department. The report also sets out very clearly how to apply the method.

The technique stems from the survival curve of the type already shown in Fig. 4.1. It accords with common sense that one can expect the highest peak of leaving to occur shortly after joining, when staff find whether or not they like the job and the company finds out whether or not they are suitable. The type of job will affect the time interval between joining and this peak. For an unskilled job, it may be a matter of a few weeks or even less, whereas for executive staff it might be two or three years. Nevertheless, one can be fairly confident that the shape of the curve will be the same—log-normal—in both cases. It can be useful merely to draw such curves; for an aim of manpower planning might be to 'stretch out' the curve, i.e. to move the peak to the right so that such a large number of losses does not occur early in the life of the cohort.

It is perhaps worth explaining for the non-statistician how the curve in Fig. 4.3 is transformed into a straight line. The first step is to use a logarithmic scale for the time interval (Fig. 4.4). This gives the familiar 'normal' curve. The next step is to plot this curve with the cumulative number of leavers, or percentage of the original cohort who have left (Fig. 4.5). Finally, by use of a 'normal' or 'probability' scale for the vertical axis, this becomes a straight line (Fig. 4.6). It will be clear that

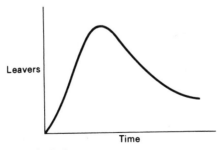

FIG. 4.3   Cohort analysis 1

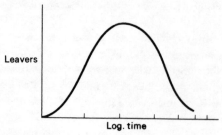

FIG. 4.4   Cohort analysis 2

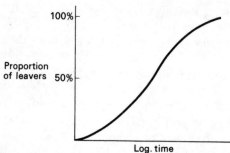

FIG. 4.5   Cohort analysis 3

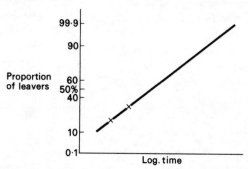

FIG. 4.6   Cohort analysis 4

one can plot survivors rather than leavers and in this case the final straight line will slope the other way.

It is, of course, possible to plot data directly on to log-probability graph paper. It should be noted that fitting the line to the points is not absolutely straightforward because the non-linearity of the coordinates of the graph precludes the direct use of regression analysis, but in many practical cases, the fitting of the line by eye will suffice. This is, after all, what Lane and Andrew did.

The comparison of different groups is made easy by the possibility of superimposing the different lines. A method of summarising the information has been suggested by D. T. Bryant [6] and this is the *half-life*, the time taken for a cohort to be reduced to half its original size. Whilst not a way of expressing all the information given by a curve, it can be a useful way of conveying the important aspects of it.

Census method

To overcome some of the problems of the cohort method, the census method can be adopted. This was also analysed by Lane and Andrew [3] and possesses similar characteristics to the cohort method. Instead of examining one cohort over a period of time, a 'snapshot' of the total situation is taken for one, relatively short period of time. The completed length of service of leavers in (for example) one year is plotted as a histogram (Fig. 4.7). As can be seen, this gives the same form of curve

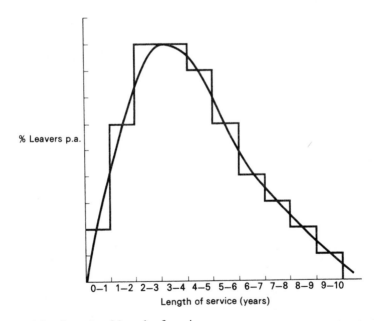

FIG. 4.7   Completed length of service

as the cohort analysis. In effect, it has achieved the combination of a number of cohorts, as required to overcome the cohort analysis problem already discussed. Indeed, it has an advantage beyond this. Since it uses only recent data (e.g. last year's), it may well be more accurate than the use of data extending back over the life of the separate cohorts.

Although the diagram shows equal length of service periods, of one year each, it is not necessary to use equal periods, since the proportion of leavers is expressed as a per annum rate. Therefore it is possible to take shorter periods, of perhaps three months each, at the beginning of the length of service spectrum, and periods of more than one year at the end of the spectrum. Provided that the periods are spaced on the horizontal axis appropriately, the same curve will be produced.

The whole manpower system, as analysed by Lane and Andrew [3], is described by four functions:

The number of men engaged between times t_1 and t_2.

Probability of entrant at time t leaving with a length of service between x_1 and x_2.

Number of men leaving between t_1 and t_2 with lengths of service between x_1 and x_2.

Number of men at time t with lengths of service between x_1 and x_2.

From this can be calculated another function $\phi(x)$ which gives the proportion of men who join at a given time who will survive to length of service x, i.e. a forecast of retention of staff can be made. Theoretically, and sometimes in practice, the function varies according to time of joining, but for the calculation it is assumed that $\phi(x)$ is independent of time of joining.

This function did not require calculation in the cohort analysis method, being merely the proportion surviving of the cohort after period of service x. Its calculation under the census method is shown in Table 4.1.

Retention profile

Somewhat akin to the census method is the retention profile. This method has the advantage that it is a little simpler to use and to understand. This may be important to the personnel manager both for his own sake in using it, and because he has to explain and make use of his techniques in cooperation with line managers and the top management

TABLE 4.1   Census method: probability of leaving

Length of service	Manning			Leavers	Turnover % p.a.	δ_r	$\phi(x)$ as percentage
	Start of year	End of year	Average				
0–3 m	184	292	238	406	170·59	0·4265	65·3
3–6 m	175	132	153·5	128	83·39	0·2085	53·0
6–9 m	152	157	154·5	53	34·30	0·0858	48·6
9–12 m	176	153	164·5	45	27·36	0·0864	45·4
1–2 yr	390	463	426·5	75	17·58	0·1758	38·1
2–5 yr	1235	1147	1191·0	169	14·19	0·4257	24·9
5–10 yr	732	837	784·5	56	7·14	0·3570	17·4
10–15 yr	1616	1459	1537·5	61	3·97	0·1985	14·3
15–20 yr	785	795	790	26	3·29	0·1645	12·1
20 yr	1722	1690	1706·0	61	3·58	—	—

$$\delta_r = \frac{I_r}{100} l_r$$

where, I_r = turnover rate p.a. for the rth length of service group.

l_r = length of the rth interval, i.e. the first four intervals are 0·25 of a year, the fifth is one year etc.

and

$$\log_e \phi(x_r) \approx \log_e \phi(x_{r-1}) - \delta_r$$

or

$$\log_{10} \phi(x_r) \approx \log_{10} \phi(x_{r-1}) - \frac{\delta_r}{2 \cdot 3026}$$

Note. $\phi(x_r)$ = percentage remaining after completing service of x years/months. Source: Lane and Andrew [3].

of his organisation. While there is often an unwarranted tendency for executive staff to believe that their senior management cannot understand techniques which have any complexity at all, it is nevertheless important to take account of the problems of communicating a complex system to them and to balance this against the degree of accuracy required in forecasting. It must be remembered that it is necessary for top management to appreciate the nature of the forecasts, because they have to make decisions resulting from them.

The retention profile, whilst it loses something in accuracy compared with the cohort analysis and census methods, is readily understood and is also easy to put into use, having only simple data requirements. It is almost certainly a better guide to the changing morale of the organisation than the labour turnover index and is in a form which can be applied directly to manpower forecasting.

On the assumption that manpower forecasts will normally be made for periods of one year, the analysis of retention of staff is based on annual patterns and the rates of retention found can be applied to the forecast for each successive year. The emphasis is on retention, partly because this is the information required in forecasting supply but also because it puts the emphasis on retaining staff rather than losing them. It is hoped that this engenders a more positive attitude to problems of labour turnover: it certainly draws attention to the need to retain staff at least for that minimum period necessary to recoup initial costs.

Retained staff at the end of the year are divided into groups or cohorts by their year of joining and the number in each group is expressed as a percentage of the number who could have been retained from that cohort, i.e. all who joined in that particular year. An example of how this can be set out is given in Table 4.2; in it, normal retirements are shown separately. In effect, they are removed from the system, because for all except the longest planning periods normal retirements can be forecast in the straightforward way of examining the ages of staff. (This is probably satisfactory, normally, although in forecasting it could lead to the 'double counting' of deaths shortly before retirement or early retirements.)

The profile can be presented graphically, printed out by a computer if personnel records are computerised, as shown in Fig. 4.8. In this way, profiles for different years or different departments can be compared.

An example of a forecasting model based on the retention profile is given later in chapter 7.

TABLE 4.2   Retention profile

Manpower category 281	Length of service at end of year (years) A	Number of staff at end of year B	Normal retirements in year C	Leavers in year (excluding col. C) D	Retention rates (%) $\dfrac{B}{D+B} \times 100$ E
Sex	< 1	80	NIL	40	66·6
M	2	40	NIL	40	50·0
	3	50	NIL	30	62·5
	4	40	NIL	10	80·0
	5	25	NIL	5	83·3
	6	20	1	4	83·3
	7	12	NIL	2	85·7
	> 7	15	4	2	88·2

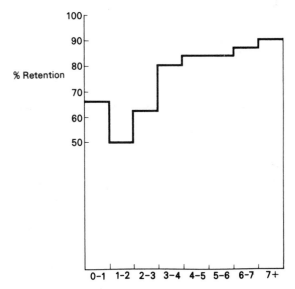

FIG. 4.8   Retention profile

ANALYSIS OF INTERNAL MOVEMENTS

So far we have been considering the movements of staff out of the man-power systems as a whole and its converse, the retention of staff within the system. However, this is only part of the internal manpower supply forecast, for the retained staff change. Some will be promoted, a few may be demoted, and others will move sideways: all these can be called *movements between categories*. Each movement out of a category will, of course, be balanced by a movement into category. It may also be that there are several divisions within the company and *transfers* between them need to be tracked. Taking the company as a whole, the *transfers in* will match the *transfers out*, but this will not necessarily be so for a particular division. (It may be interesting in itself to know which divisions are net importers and which net exporters.)

A complication may arise from the fact that 'transfers' may at the same time be 'movements between categories'. It will normally be necessary to decide which takes precedence. However, the very fact that transfers are being analysed suggests that the divisions are being treated as partly autonomous entities. Therefore, usually 'transfers' will be recorded as such, whether or not a change of category is involved. Movements between categories will thus be confined to movements within the division. In this way, the balance of movements in and out within the division is maintained.

Age and length of service distributions

Age and length of service distributions are fairly common 'tools' of personnel management. It is worth considering, however, how valuable they are. Age distributions seem somehow to imply that there is an 'ideal age distribution' which the department or company should match. Even if this were true, it is not known what it is. However, in the absence of any more sophisticated system an age analysis will show up some possible future problems. For example, a large cluster of staff nearing retirement could present problems, although it would probably be necessary to forecast the likelihood of other leavers in the same period really to know how serious the problem is. If promotions tend to be at a certain age from a group being analysed, peaks before this age could present difficulties; there may be insufficient jobs for them to go into. To know how serious this is, one must have the facts about promotion patterns, and also about the future vacancies in the higher grade.

Thus age distributions may indicate the need for further analysis, but are rarely useful in themselves, although occasionally they have a use in a non-manpower planning context; for example, in costing life assurance as a fringe benefit for staff.

Length of service distributions may have similar uses; for example, they would facilitate costing changes in holiday entitlement if the length of holiday were dependent on length of service. They are relevant to manpower planning only if the length of service of leavers is related to them. By itself a length of service distribution tells very little. It may also be relevant to promotion patterns, if length of service (or length of service in a grade) is a major determinant of promotion. In one major bank a recruitment ban over a period gave rise to a serious problem of promotion to branch manager level many years later. This might perhaps have been anticipated at the time of the ban or could have been noticed later by observing a 'gap' in the service distribution.

Such problems are difficult to deal with unless foreseen. Promoting at younger ages, even if satisfactory from the work point of view, creates an expectancy amongst staff lower down the ladder for earlier promotion which will be disappointed. If foreseen, however, various solutions are possible, ranging from reorganisation through judicious recruitment (though this has dangers of disturbing morale) to the simple expedient of retentions after retiring age.

Markov chain

One method of analysing promotion patterns is the use of the Markov Chain model. The detail of the probability theory involved will not be explained here, but can be found in Professor D. J. Bartholomew's book [7]. It is set out here in sufficient detail for the manpower planner or manager to judge whether or not it would be a helpful technique in his own context.

Figure 4.9 illustrates an organisation with a simple grade structure of three grades. It also takes three length of service groupings into account. A man recruited into Grade 3 will enter, as the arrow shows, into the box marked A. He may then remain in that grade, in which case after three years he automatically enters the 3–10 year box, marked B. He may alternatively, as the vertical arrow shows, be promoted to Grade 2 within his first three years or (along the diagonal arrow) after serving three years in Grade 1. In the figure, staff enter at Grade 2 or 3, but never at Grade 1: this grade is filled entirely by promotion from within.

It will not be difficult, if records are suitable, to discover what proportion of staff in each of the grade/service blocks moved along the different arrows in the figure. There is, of course, another movement not shown in the figure, and that is movement out of the system altogether, i.e. labour turnover. This can obviously occur from any block.

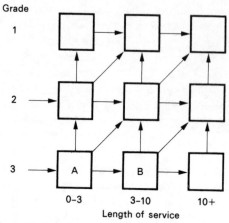

FIG. 4.9   Markov Chain

These proportions can be regarded as the probability of a man moving along the arrow to which it applies. These probabilities can be set out in a table like Table 4.3.

The table is interesting in itself. In a given year, 8 per cent of Grade 3 staff with 0–3 years' service are promoted, 5 per cent remaining in this length of service group and 3 per cent being promoted as they reach their fourth year (these two figures are ringed); but 25 per cent of them leave, as shown by the wastage vector at the bottom. Similar interesting facts are illustrated for other groups. It will be noted that most figures fall in a diagonal band. One figure outside this shows that 1 per cent of Grade 3 staff after 4–6 years' service move from Grade 3 to 1, clearly high-flyers.

The model can be used in two ways. With a fixed intake of recruits, one can calculate how the grade structure will change. Alternatively, one can forecast separately the total size of the company, and then fix the recruit numbers for each successive period in the forecast, taking wastage into account. Then, the grade structure can be calculated. In the real situation, of course, the grade structure is usually fixed, at least within limits and cannot necessarily accept promotions, or the lack of them, according to past patterns. The model can, firstly, forecast the extent of the problems attendant upon such a situation. It shows the extent to which past patterns will give rise to problems. It is then possible to use the model to calculate the effect of different flows. Thus, one could halve the number of recruits or slow down the rate of promotion.

TABLE 4.3   Markov Chain probability matrix

		3			2			1		+~
		0–3	4–6	6+	0–3	4–6	6+	0–3	4–6	6+	
3	0–3	0·52									0·85
	4–6	0·15	0·72								0
	6+		0·06	0·07							0
2	0–3	0·05			0·55						0·15
	4–6	0·03	0·05		0·20	0·76					0
	6+		0·01	0·00		0·08	0·70				0
1	0–3				0·03			0·60			0
	4–6		0·01		0·02	0·05		0·25	0·76		0
	6+					0·01	0·00		0·04	0·70	0
w~		0·25	0·15	0·30	0·20	0·10	0·30	0·15	0·20	0·30	

This table is derived from one presented in a paper to the Manpower Society by Andrew Forbes.

The usefulness of such calculations has been demonstrated, for example, by Professor Andrew Young [8]. The successive application of the transition probabilities shows the number or proportion in each grade (he uses the term *status* to express each 'block' in the Markov Chain). He shows that organisations have often achieved a state of rough equilibrium in a period of expansion. Table 4.4 shows such an organisation.

But what happens when expansion stops? The promotion pattern of the past is now expected by staff. Indeed, it may continue for a while, because the managers making the promotions follow the past pattern which seems 'fair' to them. The extent of the problem is in Table 4.5. The lowest status is shrinking, whilst the highest is increasing rapidly.

Professor Young has nicely illustrated the effect of this situation and how it can affect wastage rates. Figure 4.10 shows three *status profiles*.

In (a), each successively high status, represented by the horizontal bars, is smaller. In (b), expansion has ceased, but promotion rates have failed to react. Finally, in (c), the bulge in (b) has moved up, but the

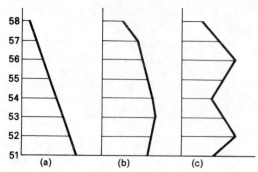

FIG. 4.10 Status profiles (reproduced from *Aspects of Manpower Planning*, EUP, 1971)

TABLE 4.4 Status profiles—with expansion

Year	Proportion in each status %							Annual expansion
	1	2	3	4	5	6	7	
1959	34·7	25·1	17·1	11·2	7·8	3·8	0·3	11
1960	36·8	23·3	17·9	10·2	7·8	3·1	0·9	18
1961	36·2	23·9	17·1	10·4	8·4	3·1	0·9	14
1962	35·4	24·1	17·2	11·0	8·1	3·2	1·0	8
1963	33·3	24·7	17·8	11·6	8·1	3·4	1·1	4
1964	33·1	23·7	18·0	12·0	8·5	3·5	1·2	8
1965	33·2	23·2	17·5	12·2	8·7	3·7	1·5	6

TABLE 4.5 Status profiles—expansion stops

Year	Proportion in each status %						
	1	2	3	4	5	6	7
1965	33·2	23·2	17·5	12·2	8·7	3·7	1·5
1966	30·4	23·7	18·1	12·9	9·3	3·9	1·7
1967	28·3	23·6	18·6	13·5	9·9	4·1	2·0
1970	24·5	22·0	19·1	14·9	11·8	4·9	2·8
Limit	20·5	16·9	14·9	13·2	14·2	8·5	11·8

(Tables 4.4 and 4.5 are reproduced from Professor Young's paper [8].)

promotion rate to the middle status levels has been cut. Realising the effect on their promotion prospects, those in the lowest status levels have begun to leave. Professor Young has named the situation in (b) and (c) the Braddock–Bardot cycle.

Renewal theory models

The basis of the Markov Chain model is fixed transition probabilities and a forecast of the resultant grades, which naturally vary in size. Reversing this calculation in the Markov Chain model, so that the grade sizes are fixed, is, in fact, mathematically rather difficult. The renewal theory model works normally in this way, i.e. the grade sizes are fixed and set the constraints of the forecasts made.

This model derives from the assumption that each individual in the organisation has a certain probability of leaving at a given time. This probability would be expected to follow the log-normal distribution discussed earlier in the chapter. It is then possible to determine the probability of each individual's leaving at a series of intervals into the future: one might, for example, work in months or weeks, counting all who leave within the month or week as leaving at the same time. By summing the probabilities of leaving of each individual at a given time, one can arrive at the proportion leaving at that time. It will be clear that if all the individuals started at the same time, the proportion leaving at any time will be the same as the probability distribution for each individual. The proportion of leavers is thus likely to follow a log-normal distribution. However, if, as in the real situation, recruitment dates vary, the probabilities of individuals may be expected to follow this distribution, but the sum of them over a series of points of time will be distributed quite differently. The model continues into the future by assuming new recruits as others leave.

So far the model has been concerned with wastage, and the assumption has been that wastage depends on length of service. The model can be extended to cover a number of grades, and in this case one of two assumptions (based, of course, on analysis of the past) has to be made:

(a) Probability of leaving depends on company length of service (as was assumed in the Markov Chain model above);
(b) Probability of leaving depends on length of service in the grade (an assumption which is not viable in the Markov Chain model).

It is also necessary to specify how an individual is selected for promotion. The promotion rule may be:

(a) that the most senior member of the grade below is selected (which will, of course, have a chain reaction down to the lowest grade, where a recruit will be taken in);

(b) that promotion occurs randomly, which approximates to the situation when merit predominates over experience in determining promotability.

The theory for these sets of assumptions has been developed by Professor Bartholomew [7].

The model will thus reveal the promotion probabilities as they change over time, and also forecast the recruitment patterns. It could, therefore, be regarded as complementary to the Markov Chain model, which forecasts grade sizes with fixed promotion probabilities.

A convenient way of regarding the two models has been given in the 1972 report of the Institute of Manpower Studies [9].

The Markov or 'Push' type models assume that promotions are not dependent on vacancies occurring, but instead are the result of management 'pushing' individuals along their career paths at fixed rates. . . . At the other extreme the Renewal or 'Pull' type models assume that all promotions are the result of vacancies occurring, as if employees are 'pulled' through the organisation to fill gaps as they arise.

In fact, as IMS points out, the real situation is usually a mixture of 'push' and 'pull' and they are now working on models which combine both elements.

Stationary population models (actuarial technique)

Another way of looking at promotion patterns is the stationary population model, which is particularly applicable in organisations with clearly defined grade structures, offering a full career. It is not surprising, therefore, that it has been particularly developed in the Ministry of Defence and has been explained, for example, by E. Jones [10]. The method uses 'service tables' which are adaptations of the life tables used by actuaries.

Table 4.6 shows a service table using a constant wastage rate. Column b shows how an intake of 1,000 declines over the years, while column e shows the net effect of recruiting 1,000 each year for 1, 2, 3 years and so on. It has, however, already been argued that a crude wastage rate of the kind used in this table can be misleading. Similar tables can be constructed for wastage patterns which are dependent on length of service. Also, different tables can be used for different grades. Such a table is given as Table 4.7.

TABLE 4.6   Service table: constant wastage rate (Wastage rate of 10 per cent p.a. of numbers at beginning of year)

Year a	Number of survivors at beginning of year b	Losses in year c	Average number in post d	Cumulative mean strength e
1	Intake = 1000	100	950	950
2	900	90	855	1805
3	810	81	769·5	2575·5

TABLE 4.7   Service table: wastage dependent on service

Year	Number of survivors at beginning of year	Losses in year	Average number in post	Cumulative mean strength
1	1000	667	667	667
2	333	167	250	917
3	166	50	141	1058
4	116	29	102	1160
5	87	17	78	1238
6	70	5	68	1306
7	65	65	33	1339
8	0			

(Source. Based on table by J. A. Rowntree in *Some Statistical Techniques of Manpower Planning* [5].)

Using these tables, one can very simply demonstrate diagrammatically how an intake dwindles from its original size of 1,000 to 500 over a period of (in this example) thirty years, as in Fig. 4.11a. This may be viewed as one entry over time. In this case, time moves up the diagram each 'layer' representing five years. Alternatively, each 'layer' can be regarded as the survivors from successive intakes, and thus the whole 'block' represents the total staff. This is true when the intake is constant and when the system has been running long enough to be in equilibrium or a 'steady state'; it thus has a stationary population.

If the block represents the total population, and if there are two grades of fixed size, then one can show the two grades as in Fig. 4.11b. This diagram is based on the policy of promoting everyone into the upper grade, and the line across the block will automatically indicate the average length of service at which promotion will be achieved. But

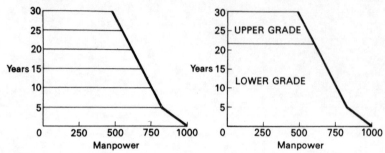

FIG. 4.11a   Stationary population model

FIG. 4.11b   Stationary population model (with grades shown)

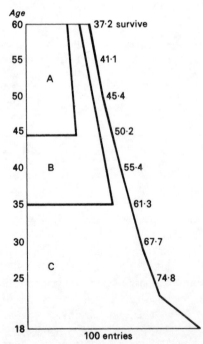

FIG. 4.12   Three grade structure shown as stationary population model

it is not usual for everyone to be promoted. For example, some may be promoted from Grade C to Grade B and others remain in Grade C. Some of the Grade B will be further promoted to Grade A. Figure 4.12, which is reproduced from a paper to a Manpower Society study panel by E. Jones [11] shows this situation. This diagram also shows wastage decreasing as length of service rises.

With such models, alternative basic strategies for promotion can be tried. One can see, for example, at what age promotions must take place if a given proportion of an intake is to be promoted. Alternatively, if promotion is to be achieved at a given length of service, the proportion achieving it is readily seen.

Their usefulness lies in the readiness with which such alternatives can be tried and the simplicity of the method of expressing possibilities to senior management. However, they will be useful only in organisations which have clearcut career patterns and which can meaningfully consider the sort of alternatives suggested above. The typical company possibly has no likelihood of ever reaching the steady state. Since the model assumes constant size, it will not be very helpful if the company is prone to large variations. Even so, unless it is very far from achieving a steady state, it may be instructive to see what the basic promotion pattern would be.

As well as using the service tables for constructing such models, they can be used for forecasting wastage and resultant recruitment. This, in effect, is the same as the use of the retention profile discussed above.

Salary progression curves

The techniques described so far have been imported into manpower planning from other fields not directly connected with company manpower problems. An importation from personnel management itself is the use of salary curves to forecast status levels in the future.

In constructing a predictive model of staff in a division of Imperial Chemical Industries Ltd, Charles Walmsley [12] needed to predict the transition probabilities of movement from one grade to another in any given year. Salary progression curves of the log parabola type are familiar to personnel managers through the work of the Glacier Institute, and he constructed similar curves for staff in the division. (Salaries naturally have to be corrected for changing money values and standard of living. The salaries index supplies a reasonable means of doing this.) Using these curves, which show corrected salary and age, he could predict the future salary changes, and thus roughly grade, of individuals on the basis of their present age and salaries. This method has the advantage over the transition probabilities so far considered that it adapts to the particular individuals, though predictions for staff under thirty were found to be somewhat unreliable. This prediction of grade changes was combined with a prediction of retention based on length of service to produce a forecasting model of internal supply.

FORECASTING METHOD

The different methods of forecasting put different emphasis on the various factors affecting the forecast. The method must, therefore, be chosen in relation to the needs of the particular organisation. In an ideal world, this would be the criterion for selection. However, in the real world, data availability may be the major criterion. If past data for several years are not available, the cohort analysis method, however appropriate, cannot be used. Even if past data are available, unless they are divided into separate manpower categories, they may be useless.

Similarly, it is not unusual for personnel records to have all the necessary information on staff retention, but not to record the dates of change of grade or of change of department. In such cases, the Markov Chain model is impossible to construct. Just as was suggested for demand forecasts, a start should be made with the data which exists. Meanwhile, the required data can be built up.

DETERMINISTIC AND STOCHASTIC MODELS

The word 'model' has been used in describing forecasting methods without explanation. The methods described, however, will have provided a working definition. The 'model' is the reduction of what actually happens to a set of statements or mathematical equations, so that the same processes can be represented even if the values of some or all of the elements are varied. Inevitably, this reduction is a simplification of the real state of affairs. The aim is, of course, to avoid an over-simplification—to retain the factors which have a major effect (for example, length of service in a model of labour turnover) and to ensure that factors excluded are relatively insignificant (such as, perhaps, number of children in the same model). The exclusions may be made because data are not available. They may also be made to obtain a simplification for its own sake. We understand the world through a series of simplifications: this is how we organise our thought. The forecasting models are ways of interpreting and understanding the processes going on in organisations.

The models may be broadly classified into two types, 'deterministic' and 'stochastic'. The basic difference is that the deterministic model deals with averages and provides no method of measuring the degree of probability of the predicted outcome. This is, therefore, a further simplification of the real world and may be acceptable for similar reasons to those for constructing the model itself. However, it is obviously true that one cannot predict human behaviour with the absolute certainty implied by such models. The stochastic model, at the expense of complication, introduces a measure of the uncertainty: it is based on probabilities rather than averages.

The difference may be regarded as one of degree. The forecasting methods, for supply and demand, described above are in the main capable of refinement to provide measures of probability. However, the measures may be ignored, so that they are used as deterministic models. On the other hand, the difference is very real: the deterministic model can be seen as a discontinuity in the progressive simplification of the real world into the series of equations of the model.

It depends on one's view of psychology, and possibly religion, whether one believes that human actions are wholly explicable. However, it must be generally accepted that a large number of factors affect the way a particular human being acts, and thus the way a particular group of human beings acts. In order to understand and predict, we simplify. In simplifying, we eliminate the less important factors: these factors are then regarded as being part of the 'random' element, which is a group of minor factors, whose explanatory nature is sufficiently small for us to be prepared not to identify them separately, with or without the inclusion in the group of a truly random element. If one believes that human actions are totally explicable there will be no truly random element, although there may be factors which one cannot, in fact, explain: on the other hand, if one believes that one cannot explain human actions entirely, the unexplained element can be characterised as 'random', which is to say inexplicable.

Thus the random element (which is what reduces the certainty of a deterministic model to the probability of a stochastic model) contains all the factors which we cannot identify or have elected not to identify; but the major factors and the random element are the total of all the influences on the model. As one simplifies, the major factors are reduced and the random element increased.

In the deterministic model, the choice is made to neglect the random element. Thus, some of the influences on the model are ignored completely. In this sense, it is a radically different type of model. However, this is not to say that its use is not justified in many circumstances where simplicity is important.

The difference between the two types has an important effect on the results obtained from the models. The deterministic model, because it works with averages, gives results as averages. This means that it probably gives results in fractions of men. For presentation to management, this is not ideal. The stochastic model, however, attempts to simulate the actual processes. This means that one can not only trace the processes as they happen in the model, but also the computer will itself produce a typical result which is 'real', i.e. is in a form which actually *could* happen.

5

External manpower supply

The manpower demand forecast has been made. The internal manpower supply forecast has been made. Unless the company is approaching a period of contraction in manpower demand or a great increase in productivity, there is likely to be a shortfall in supply. Immediately, attention will be turned to the external supply of manpower. Will it be possible to recruit?

EXTERNAL SUPPLY AND DEMAND

The importance of this element in planning is being increasingly recognised by management, certainly in short-term plans for relocated or new factories. It is no use moving to a new site where communications are good, if you will not be able to staff the factory. Furthermore, it is no use moving to the North-East, for example, even if labour in general is readily available, unless the *type of labour* required is present. Many firms moving to areas of high unemployment have found to their cost that craftsmen are even more difficult to recruit than they were at their previous location. It is in recognition of this problem that the 'Key Workers' Scheme' was set up by the then Ministry of Labour, to provide grants to workers moved to development areas, if they were in such 'key' positions. A similar situation can obtain even in the current period of high unemployment.

It hardly needs any illustrations to emphasise how greatly the external supply can affect planning decisions. Yet it can so easily be forgotten, as it has been by some firms moving to development areas. A clear example is provided by a large organisation who decided to enlarge their R and D effort. Their resultant requirement for PhD physicists in their university recruitment programme was seen by the manpower planners to be greater than the expected output of all British universities in that year. Plans were thus modified before they had gone too far.

In this case, external supply information was available. This is rarely the case. The problem is compounded by the fact that the manpower planner in a company requires two types of external information. He needs to know the future size of the work force, in the category and the region with which he is concerned (the 'supply'), and he also needs to know the competition for this supply from other employers (the 'demand').

He may find some figures available on the supply side if he digs for them, but they may be so general as to be useless. Regular forecasts of the total population are made and appear in the *Monthly Abstract of Statistics*. From time to time, with this basis, the Department of Employment provides, in the *Department of Employment Gazette*, forecasts of the working population. The translation of population into working population depends on a number of assumptions, the prime of which is the 'activity rate', the proportion of particular age and sex groups who will be employed [1]. (There is an interaction between supply and demand here: the activity rate of married women, for example, drops in times of low demand and, in effect, absorbs a good deal of reduced employment levels before they begin to show in the unemployment figures.) This is one of the very few relevant figures which is predictive.

Regional employment figures provide historic data, but no forecasts. Occupational figures are also historic only. Furthermore, they are not by any means comprehensive. Self-employed workers are omitted entirely. So, for most purposes, are most workers in non-manufacturing industry. For example, the annual survey of occupational structure, which in any case concentrates on craftsmen, was restricted entirely to manufacturing, and is now further restricted to engineering.

Most of these figures are the responsibility of the Department of Employment; some are published by the Ministry of Agriculture, the Department of the Environment or the Department of Trade and Industry.

Apart from the survey of certain occupations in manufacturing, the figures provided are better described as industrial than occupational. Comprehensive occupational figures come only from the Census of Population, which means that they are well out-of-date when they appear and are in themselves suspect, because they result from self-classification by the population generally.

The need for detailed figures within an industry may be provided by the Industrial Training Board: many Training Boards have given considerable attention to the need to forecast manpower demands in order to establish training requirements. The company manpower planner, however, may be less interested in the forecasts for his own industry than for his own region, for many workers will be interchangeable in some degree. The independence of training boards and the lack of any genuinely coordinating body has meant that there has been no means of bringing manpower statistics together from different boards nor, indeed, of ensuring their compatibility.

This failure is unfortunate, because the importance of training boards to manpower planning is considerable. If a board aims to increase training, it is important that it is clear by how much and for what manpower categories an increase in training is desirable. This means, implicitly or explicitly, that manpower forecasts are needed. Many ITBs have recognised the need explicitly and have set forecasting work in hand. Just as important, however, has been their spreading of knowledge to firms about the need for forecasting and planning, both through their direct communications and through the members of the boards themselves, who come from industry and from trade unions. Although training boards have not had any direct means of increasing or altering training, since the levy-grant system provides no incentives [2], the attention directed to training has affected it, and brought the planning of it to the attention of the boards of companies.

The Manpower Research Unit, set up in 1964 within the Ministry of Labour, promised at first to produce some information of use to manpower planners. They began by analysing the past and present manpower in various industries. Although rarely able to forecast, they did appear to be setting the groundwork for forecasts and, possibly, for improved statistics. However, the impetus for their work seemed to fall off quite rapidly and their apparent output dwindled, although official bodies and government ministers continued to expect from them reports and forecasts for all industries, as has been commented on in chapter 1 [3 and 4]. The report on the Central Training Council also made the point that there was a need for greater coordination, but offered no solution other than a greater involvement of the MRU. The situation has remained that there has been no coordination and many statistics have not been available. The Central Training Council was an advisory body with no coordinating function and the MRU was submerged in internal reorganisations in the Department of Employment.

The establishment of the Training Services Agency in 1973, however, will doubtlessly lead to this coordination which has been lacking for so long.

COLLECTION AND COORDINATION OF STATISTICS

This lack of coordination of statistics and of the work of the training boards, together with the complete absence of statistics required for company manpower planning, cries out for the formation of a body which will carry out the task. Various suggestions have been made for a National Manpower Commission or a similar body: see, for example, the Edinburgh Group report [5]. At about the same time (1967) Edward Heath, then in opposition, called for such a body, and now Clive Jenkins, general secretary of the Association of Scientific, Technical and Managerial Staff, is making similar proposals, basing them on the Swedish example, the National Labour Market Board. A very similar proposal, stemming directly from a study of Industrial Training Boards, has also been made by PEP [6]. The Institute of Personnel Management has also made representations to the Government in a similar vein.

At the time of writing the Government has just announced the establishment of a 'Manpower Services Commission', but it is not clear that this body will fulfil the needs set out here. Its brief at the moment does not seem to go beyond running the Employment Service and the Training Services Agency, whereas the National Manpower Commission envisaged by these various bodies would coordinate and extend statistics relating to the labour market. Such a body would also be concerned with manpower forecasts at the national or 'macro' level, but it is forecasts of occupational categories and regional manpower, both supply and overall demand, which the company requires.

A main aim of Swedish macro-level manpower forecasting is to plan the educational system appropriately, and in some developing countries planning education is geared very tightly to anticipated needs, so that only those qualifications expected to be 'useful' are obtained. In the UK, however, Lord Robbins's Committee on Higher Education [7] decided that such planning was impossible and that education facilities should provide the course which people want, without reference to the country's needs. There does even seem to be a view that it is actually undesirable and a denial of freedom to plan the provision of courses by reference to the country's needs. Yet many undergraduates have no very firm view, when they begin their courses, about the subjects they wish to study. Whilst not denying the right of those really keen to read Sanskrit, it seems senseless to encourage others to read Sanskrit by supplying the places to do so, when by different provision some of them could be encouraged to read a subject leading to work in areas where the country is expected to need them.

For the company manpower planner, as the physicist example showed, educational statistics may be useful in themselves. Here, detailed historic figures are available in the Department of Education and Science's annual statistics. Forecasts are less easy to come by, although much work is going on in, for example, the Higher Education Research Unit at the London School of Economics. Nevertheless, it was impossible in the summer of 1970 to discover how many students would graduate, by subjects, in 1970, although they had been at university three years by then, and certainly no forecasts for future years were available.

Figures on school-leavers may also be relevant. It would make an interesting study to see how many companies anticipated the effects of the raising of the school-leaving age.

THE LOCAL LABOUR MARKET

Faced with this situation, the company manpower planner must make do with what information he can get. He will know trends in the working population. He knows how easy or difficult it is to recruit currently and he may be able to guess how things will change. He may be able to learn of new factories or factory closures in his area. New housing estates may mean more workers. The local employment exchange manager can be a mine of useful information on these and related matters. A good manager keeps very closely in touch with all the employers in his area.

However, the Department of Employment is not well prepared for such requests.[1] Not long ago a company planning a major expansion of a factory enquired of the local office for advice. The Department assured the personnel manager that everything would be all right, but, when pressed, made it clear that what they meant was that planning permission would almost certainly be granted, because the factory was in a 'corridor of industrial development'. They disclaimed all knowledge

[1] The Department of Employment has been running a project on 'local labour market intelligence' in some pilot areas, with the aim of helping to provide relevant information to companies, and results seem to be encouraging.

of the employment situation ! And the corridor of development was in an area with an existing shortage of labour, rather strange in itself. At present, however, it is with such minimal indications of future trends that the manpower planner must be content in assessing the possibilities of future recruitment.

It is disappointing that no real improvement is planned in the collection, interpretation and general provision of national, regional and industrial manpower data. The blueprint for the future of the employment service, *People and Jobs* [8], makes little more than a gesture towards the need for more manpower information, placing the emphasis on regional manpower demand. There is no recognition of the need for coordination of all manpower statistics and of the total lack of some, such as local manpower supply. The earlier consultative document had not covered this need either, but had talked of 'manpower centres' rather than 'employment offices', carrying an implication of this kind of extension of the service.

This is not to say that the provision of these statistics would make the situation absolutely clear. It has been demonstrated that the labour market is very far from 'perfect'. Derek Robinson has shown that there are wide variations in the rates paid in one locality for the same job and that there is thus no direct relationship between level of wages and labour supply [9]. In fact, workpeople often do not know what rates are being paid elsewhere, so they can hardly respond to them.

An insight into some of the factors involved is provided by Dan Gowler [10]. Figure 5.1, reproduced from his article, shows how market demands affect product changes (arrow a) and these in turn effect changes in production arrangements (arrow b), job requirements (arrow c) and hence labour demand (arrow d). But that is not the end of the story, as might appear from some manpower planning work. Arrows e–j represent what Gowler calls the 'dynamic of the manufacturing situation'. Job requirements affect job expectations, but unless the job measures up to the expectations of the workforce it will not be filled (arrow e). And expectations may include 'social satisfaction' as well as pay and conditions. Naturally, expectations are modified in a tight labour market situation, but the labour market is also modified by the expectations of the workers in it (arrows f and g). Finally, if the demand for labour is not satisfied, the job requirements may have to be modified (arrow h) and thus the production arrangement and product programme (arrows i and j).

Nevertheless, without the basic manpower data, even the crudest assessment of external manpower supply cannot be attempted and one is thrown back on intelligent guesses, with perhaps a certain amount of supporting evidence.

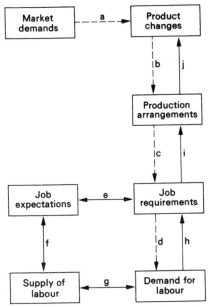

FIG. 5.1   General model of labour supply (reproduced from *Determinants of the Supply of Labour to the Firm*)

6

The manpower plan

The manpower plan is the action plan resulting from the various analyses and forecasts. It seems hardly worth saying that all the work of forecasting is wasted if no action programme stems from it; yet this is often the point at which manpower planning breaks down. Perhaps this is because it is at this point that the process moves from the hands of the specialist manpower planner to the hands of general management. The manpower planner may advise on the action needed, but he cannot take the final decisions which involve inter-relationships with resources other than manpower. This is the task of general management, using the information supplied to him by the manpower planner and, of course, by other specialists as well. The advice he receives may be incompatible and a reconciliation must be achieved.

If the changeover from the planner is to be achieved smoothly, the manager must understand something of the underlying methods; for he may have to adapt and change the forecasts and advice to achieve the reconciliation. Equally, the planner must realise the kind of changes which may be necessary and present his forecasts and tentative plans accordingly. Furthermore, it is he who must ensure that management does sufficiently understand the underlying forecasting methods.

First, to understand the interactions within the manpower planning process itself and the interactions with other resource planning, let us re-examine the manpower planning process in a little more detail than in chapter 2.

Figure 6.1 represents the forecasting process and the cycle of decisions involved. It will be noticed that it is an elaboration of the diagram used earlier (Fig. 2.1). The manpower demand forecast stems from the objectives of the organisation as represented in the business plan. Alongside this is the forecast of internal supply stemming from an

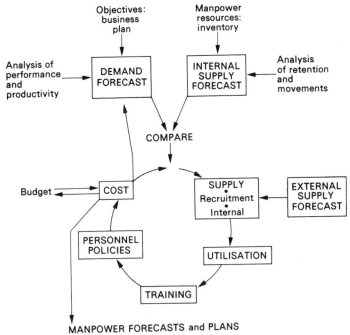

FIG. 6.1   The manpower planning process

analysis of past retention and movements applied to the existing inventory of manpower resources. These two forecasts can then be compared. It is unlikely that they will match. In an expanding situation, the supply will be less than the demand. In a contracting situation, this may be true as well, but it is possible that the supply will exceed the demand.

MANPOWER SUPPLY

Then the decision cycle begins. In the expanding situation, attention will first be given to increasing the supply. This can be done simply by recruiting and, as we have seen, information about the external labour market is required to assess the viability of this course of action. Internal means to alter the supply are also available, if, for example, the mix of skills needs to be changed. Promotion policies may need changing in the face of requirements. Transfer policies can also be amended. In this way the supply side of the equation can be changed.

There may be specific decisions to be taken on all these factors. For example, it may be necessary to mount a special recruitment campaign for a specific type of employee, which could involve an appropriate public relations campaign to build the image of the company in the area where the recruitment will be needed.

If different sources of recruitment are used to supply the same categories of manpower, it could be important to distinguish between these different sources so that the effect of the mix of sources can be assessed. For example, if graduates, school-leavers and experienced recruits combine to make up the total of entrants to the sales force, it may be important to understand their different characteristics. It may be that the effectiveness of graduates reaches a high level more quickly, but that they find that the task palls quickly and their effectiveness falls off or they leave, unless they are promoted. So a forecast of promotion prospects will be relevant to the number of graduates to be recruited. If promotion is not quickly available, it could be that it is better to have a stable, but slightly less effective, work force, thus minimising the numbers who are unproductively under training.

Salesmen are an interesting subject for the behavioural scientist. They are traditionally thought to be individualists, wanting to work on their own, yet extrovert and readily making contact with their customers. Currently research is going on to identify the characteristics of the good salesman and of the man who will wish to remain a salesman for a considerable period of time. This is one example of the way in which behavioural science research feeds information into the manpower planning process. It is trite to point to the need to improve selection and thus improve labour retention, but it may be that different mixes, like the high performance, promotable graduate instead of the long-stay school-leaver, are appropriate at different times. As research findings increase the predictability of such factors, the forecasting can be correspondingly more sophisticated.

Graduate recruitment can in itself present problems to the manpower planner; yet, it is often an area where planning is important, because of expensive recruitment campaigns and relatively high initial salaries. At one time, the high degree of competition between employers for graduates also added to the need to plan. However, the increase in output from higher education has been accompanied by a reduction in demand. Many firms have reassessed their needs and although this may have been caused by the economic recession, its effect seems likely to last after the recession has passed. The problems of graduate recruitment, however, will remain. Recruitment usually takes place in the spring, long before the graduate joins. Apart from the difficulty of recruiting someone who may never have done anything like the task for which he is being recruited, one is determining recruitment needs at least nine months before the recruits will join. Furthermore, there is no firm indication yet of his ability in his own subject either.

The long lead time is often further complicated by a training period of up to two years. If there is a graduate apprenticeship, the company may well be looking ahead to posts after two years' training, so that, with the recruitment lead time, they require a forecast of demand about three years ahead. If they really want managers, their forecast may need to be of posts to be filled in fifteen years—but it is more likely to be an act of faith on this score! However, they certainly must place them in worthwhile posts after training, both to begin to recoup training costs and to retain them for those managerial posts in which they have placed their faith.

A corollary of this sort of planning is that it is necessary not only to be able to distinguish manpower categories in analysing productivity and retention, but also 'recruit types', which might be extended to different backgrounds (e.g. which industry recruits came from) as well as the educational source, if this is relevant, or likely to be relevant, and thus worth analysing.

If the situation is one of contraction there will, of course, be different considerations. The supply forecast must be viewed cautiously. If retention is not related to length of service, the forecast is likely to be particularly misleading. With no recruitment, and thus no short-service staff, retention will quite probably 'improve', which may not be what is wanted. It may well be that natural wastage will be insufficient to effect the reduction required.

Other factors could be relevant and it may be, without previous analysable experience, that a guess must be made of their effect. If the industry is failing, morale may be low and wastage high. If the reduction results from technological advance or productivity agreements, morale may be high and wastage may remain low or even decrease.

If reductions cannot be achieved by wastage and redeployment, redundancy programmes can be planned. If this is predicted, at least all steps to minimise the effect can be taken. Whilst advance warning to unions, work force and, not least, the employment exchange is good practice, it may be that there is a need to discourage leaving until a particular time. Incentives to remain can be given, as a bonus to those still employed at a given date. Redundancy payments, made only when redundancy is actually declared, have the same effect, though care must be taken not to give notice in a way which is legally equivalent to declaring a redundancy. These measures may be sufficient, without the need to suppress information about impending redundancies, though part of the point of early warning is to allow employees to make alternative plans for themselves over a period of time.

MANPOWER UTILISATION

The next stage in the decision cycle is the examination of utilisation. If supply is less than demand one can increase the supply or decrease the demand or both. This is not the first time utilisation has been considered in the manpower planning process. In arriving at the original demand forecast, a forecast of improved productivity was taken into consideration. The justification for considering it is, however, different at this stage. In making the demand forecast, the best use of manpower was the aim. The improvement in productivity could be said to have had an economic justification. Now there is a new reason for reconsidering the matter—the 'shortage' justification. If there is insufficient manpower available, or recruitment would be difficult or costly, it may be worth considering improved productivity on a basis which in a better manpower supply position would have been considered uneconomic.

This stage in the diagram has been labelled 'utilisation' not because improvement through improved technology would not be appropriate, but because technological change involves capital investment. It is thus outside the realm of manpower decisions and is more appropriately considered at the point of interaction with other plans, represented by the budget and the business plan.

Improvement in manpower utilisation is a subject in its own right, but it is worth considering here the range of techniques and practices which may be relevant to it and thus to the manpower planner.

Of the techniques, the most obvious is work study, since it is so well established in industry, but a number of others can be used as well as or instead of it. Cost-benefit analysis is one example. There is also the whole field of work allocation. The critical path method is of special value when there are a number of projects to which resources, including manpower, can be devoted in different ways. It was developed to deal with the complexities of power station building programmes by the Central Electricity Generating Board. Indeed, in appropriate circumstances critical path analyses may be used in arriving at manpower demand forecasts.

A broader approach to the allocation of resources, when the necessity to break down the project into its component tasks does not exist, is through *linear programming*. It is worth giving some attention to this technique because it is highly adaptable and can be used in other aspects of manpower planning also.

Let us take an oversimplified example. A firm makes three products, using the same manpower and machines in the manufacture of each one. The profit on them is, however, variable. These facts can be quantified as follows:

Product	Man hours	Machine hours	Profit per unit P
A	10	10	5
B	25	20	15
C	15	5	10

Now, there could be a number of factors which prevent the company from devoting all its time to the most profitable product. For example, it has orders for 20 of product A already, but the full potential market is thought to be unlimited. For B, there are orders for 30 but the potential sales are thought to be limited to 50, whereas there are no orders for C and it is thought that only 30 can be sold in the period under consideration. These *constraints* can be expressed as:

$$A \geqslant 20 \tag{1}$$

$$50 \geqslant B \geqslant 30 \tag{2}$$

$$30 \geqslant C \tag{3}$$

Naturally, only a limited amount of machine time is available to the company, in this case 1,250 hours in the period, so that

$$10A + 20B + 5C \leqslant 1{,}250 \tag{4}$$

Manpower, on the other hand, is limited by the accommodation available to 1,500 man hours. It is not possible to have fluctuations in the work force. There is scope for reducing the hours, by cutting out overtime, to 1,200 man hours:

$$1500 \geqslant 10A + 25B + 15C \leqslant 1{,}200 \tag{5}$$

A number of mixes of product could be produced in the period, but naturally the company wants to maximise its profit. The function to be maximised is the *objective function*:

$$P = 5A + 15B + 10C \tag{6}$$

R. W. Morgan [1] has set out a simple example of the application of linear programming to supply forecasting. He gives an age distribution of two grades of staff. In five years' time all staff will have moved to the next age group, but some will be promoted from one grade to another and some age groups in the lower grade will have been supplemented by recruits. Various constraints operate on the promotion rate, the number of recruits and their ages and the age distribution of the senior grade. The aim might then be to minimise costs, minimise recruitment or maximise promotion rates. Thus, linear programming can be used in a number of aspects of manpower planning.

In distinction from techniques as a means of improving manpower utilisation, there are certain management practices. Some put the onus on managers, like management by objectives and other forms of management development. Others put the onus on the worker, for example, incentive schemes, job rotation and job enrichment. Productivity bargaining, the prevalence of which waned with the demise of the national incomes policy, was often more concerned with bargaining than with productivity, but the genuine cases could be characterised as putting the onus on worker and manager. The worker must adopt a new approach to work, perhaps undertaking tasks previously reserved for someone else, but management must give the opportunity for this to bring about improved productivity and, indeed, continually press for its achievement.

These techniques and practices are not in themselves manpower planning, but are directly relevant to it, providing an input of expected changes and being a part of the output—the way in which necessary improvements are to be achieved.

Poor utilisation of manpower may not be just the use of too many men, but also the use of the wrong sort of manpower. For example, Denis Pym has done much work examining the failure to use qualified staff properly [2].

A distinction was made implying the reverse of this problem by the Committee on Manpower Resources for Science and Technology [3] between 'need' and 'demand'. The number that industry said they wanted was called 'demand'; the number nationally desirable was called 'need'. They took the view that the need was greater than the demand. The distinction is perhaps conceptually useful, but the practical means of distinguishing the one from the other are not normally available in any objective sense. The idea that the need exceeded the demand may have failed to distinguish clearly the different levels of utilisation. Given an existing level of utilisation, it may be that need exceeds demand. Improved utilisation, however, might make the reverse true. It has been shown that 'demand' for manpower in the nuclear industry of the USA was never met; yet output of the industry outpaced all predictions. Need was apparently less than demand [4].

TRAINING

The next item, continuing round the circle in Fig. 6.1, is training. Many of the considerations here stem from the plans being formulated at the previous stages. Recruitment plans may have induction and initial training implications. Promotions imply the need for development plans. Redeployment could mean a need for retraining. All these are parts of a supply plan. Better utilisation may mean a training need as well, whether the need is to improve the quality of the work force as a whole or of the management team only.

All training is related in some way to future manpower plans. Indeed, to decide on a training programme requires a knowledge of manpower demand and supply. Writing in 1965 about manpower planning, P. R. Hodgson, then manpower planning manager at the Ford Motor Company, expressed surprise that 'the necessities of training had not mothered its invention earlier' [5].

An example of the application of forecasting to training, illustrating a number of the considerations involved was given in the Edinburgh Group report already mentioned [6]. This showed the calculations needed to estimate an apprentice intake, and the decisions which needed to be taken in determining the size of intake. These are decisions which are implicit in any overall decision on how many apprentices to recruit, although such a decision is often taken on the basis of the other factors, like the size of the training school. The example is quoted in the Edinburgh Group report's words:

Any expansion in requirements for craftsmen will probably take place more or less steadily throughout the year, whereas apprentices normally all finish at one time. Hence a conscious decision is required whether to carry a surplus for a time or make do with a deficiency until the new craftsmen are ready. However, a firm may tolerate unfilled vacancies from the beginning of the calendar year until July, when apprentices pass out, and then carry a surplus until the end of the year. In other words, the apprentices will fill craftsmen vacancies in the year during which they finish training.

Other solutions are, of course, possible. A surplus may be carried, gradually diminishing over a year, so that there is never a deficiency. Conversely, a deficiency may be carried for a year, gradually increasing until the output from the apprenticeship scheme makes up the numbers to what is really required. All this assumes a fairly steady, or steadily increasing, demand for craftsmen throughout the year. But this may not be so. There may be peaks in the need. It is when the demand for energy is low that the energy supplying industries can carry out their major maintenance work, so that they require maintenance craftsmen most in the summer. But the motor industry can re-arrange production lines when demand is low, in the winter, and thus the peak for its contractors' craftsmen will be in the winter.

The formula for determining apprentice intake is:

$$(b-a) + \left(\frac{(a+b)}{2} \times \frac{c}{100}\right) + \frac{x}{100}\left(\frac{(a+b)}{2} \times \frac{d}{100}\right) \times \frac{1}{\left(1 - \frac{e}{100}\right)^f}$$

This assumes that unfilled vacancies are tolerated up to the time of completion of apprenticeships in July.

a = establishment for December of penultimate year of training (i.e. for year from January to that December)

b = establishment for December of last year of training

c = annual hardcore turnover (percentage figure) (i.e. deaths and retirements)

d = annual voluntary turnover (percentage figure) (including dismissals)

e = annual turnover of apprentices in training (percentage figure)

f = length of apprenticeship (in years)

x = proportion (as percentage) of voluntary turnover which it is decided to train. Most of those who leave voluntarily are not losses to their trade group and training replacements for them is not necessary.

The formula is merely a summation of needs for craftsmen: expansion + hardcore turnover + a proportion of voluntary turnover. The final term is a correction for losses in training, that is, it converts the output required from the training scheme to the input needed to give this output. If apprentices leave at the rate of 5%, after four years of apprenticeship an intake of 100 apprentices will be depleted by about 18. Thus an intake of 100 is fine if requirements of craftsmen are 82. If requirements were 100, the intake would have to be 123. The accompanying figure [i.e. Fig. 6.2] illustrates this calculation.

The basis of this calculation was adopted by the Electricity Supply Industry Training Board. Industrial Training Boards happened to be set up at the time when there was a growing awareness of the need to plan manpower and many of them naturally became involved in manpower planning work. If they were to increase the volume (as well as the quality) of training, they naturally needed to know what manpower requirements were likely to be. The work of some of the ITBs has begun to build up information about particular industries, but the value is slightly diminished because it is uncoordinated, indeed inconsistent,

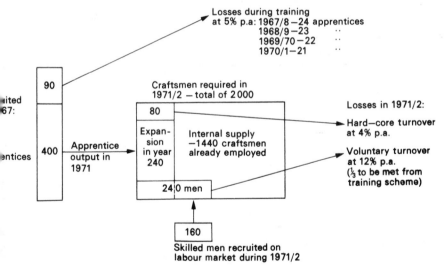

FIG. 6.2 Pattern of apprentice recruitment: recruitment of 490 is required in 1967 to supply the requirements of 1971–72. (Reproduced from *Perspectives in Manpower Planning: an Edinburgh Group Report*, IPM)

from one industry to another. More important, some of them did bring home to managements the need to plan manpower, though before that they often had to bring home the need to *plan*.

A significant fact about training boards is that they have trade union members, who were thus involved in this realisation of the need to forecast and plan. It may not be unconnected with this fact that trade unionists have in the main supported the cause of manpower planning even when it might have been, albeit misguidedly, connected in their minds with manpower savings and redundancy. They have held to the view, quite rightly, that the organisation which does not plan its manpower can be accused of callously regarding men as items of equipment to be 'bought in' and discarded as circumstances change, with no thought to them as people.

PERSONNEL POLICIES

All other personnel policies are connected with recruiting and retaining staff to a greater or less extent. They are therefore connected with manpower planning. The supply of manpower can be affected in various ways by personnel policies. Salary and wage administration ensures that market rates are paid for jobs, so that recruitment needed to fulfil the manpower demand is possible. This will also have some importance in retaining staff, though other aspects may have greater importance; for example, the suitability of the method of awarding salary increases, the general conditions of employment and the working conditions.

These are, of course, 'hygiene' factors. Possibly more important are the 'motivators'. An element in this may just be the general atmosphere, created by management, in which work is carried out. But specific policies, such as job rotation or job enrichment, may be used to alter the working situation and to maintain that alteration. Such policies may also affect utilisation, and thus manpower demand.

It is clear that the manpower planner is making assumptions about all these policies when he makes his forecasts. He may well assume their continuance unchanged. Even this has implications: the effort being put into wage market analysis, for example, must be continued. If it emerges from the manpower planning process, however, that there is a need to improve utilisation, or to improve the retention of employees, then it may well be that the organisation must turn to these policies.

It is probable that it will not be possible to quantify accurately what these policies may achieve, but the manpower plan will indicate what it is intended should be achieved. Since manpower planning is a continuous process it will be possible to monitor what is being achieved and adapt or add to the plans accordingly, as time goes on. It may even be possible to measure the effectiveness of the particular policies adopted, though it is always difficult positively to exclude the effect of other changes which are happening all the time within the organisation and in the environment.

A number of other aspects of personnel policy have already been covered. The monitoring of labour turnover and labour stability, as well as being a rough-and-ready indicator of morale, which is all that it usually is, assumes a new, further significance in the manpower planning process. It not only supplies part of the information for forecasts, but it also may need to be changed to achieve a particular part of the manpower plan.

Sickness and absenteeism in general may also be relevant. Absence, often not examined in detail by personnel departments, may have a significant effect on manpower utilisation. It may therefore be necessary to attempt to reduce it. It will certainly be necessary to monitor it, to ensure that it is not rising or fluctuating to a significant degree. Such monitoring may reveal problems of many different kinds: there may be an industrial relations problem, as there was in the Coal Board some years ago, when the unions cooperated with management in checking excessive absenteeism. There may be a work organisation problem or, possibly associated with this, a problem of job involvement and interest: it often happens, for example, that small shift teams, who are dependent on each other, have significantly less absence than day workers in larger groupings.

On the other hand, it may be recruitment that is at fault. Here the work of industrial psychology may be relevant: the work on selection methods, on fitting the job to the man and fitting the man to the job.

It will thus be seen that much, if not all, the work of industrial psychologists, and behavioural scientists in general, is relevant to manpower planning. The fact that a large part of their studies have been connected with labour turnover emphasises this fact.

INDUSTRIAL RELATIONS

Manpower planning has a significant part to play in industrial relations as well. The *Code of Industrial Relations Practice* [7] presses the importance of manpower planning, the major implication being the one already mentioned, that managements should be studying the future of their manpower and making decisions only in the light of knowledge and of clear plans. Thus redundancies may be avoided if anticipated in good time and, if not avoided, planning well in advance can enable management at least to lessen the blow. These situations, which are the effect of manpower supply exceeding demand, may entail redeployment and thus have implications for training as well as other parts of the manpower supply forecast. In judging what plans to make in such circumstances it is necessary to know the cost of recruitment of different types of staff. It will often be the case that retraining costs no more than recruiting staff directly into the vacant jobs. The cost of recruitment is also essential information in judging the significance of a particular level of labour turnover.

Apart from the possibility of redundancy, no negotiator should face a union across the table without knowing the manpower plans of his organisation. He can only judge the significance of demands and concessions in the light of future manpower needs. An extra payment to one group of employees could assume enormous significance if their numbers were to treble in the next two years, or if a reorganisation were to place them in the same department as a similar group not getting the payment. Clearly, the negotiator must know the cost implications of all proposals and the capacity of his company to pay, and to do this in the long term he must know the manpower plans of the company. It may even be that the plans need adapting as a result of negotiations. The negotiator should at least be aware of what he is causing as he makes his decisions at the negotiating table.

A more subtle, and long-term, effect of manpower planning on industrial relations might be a new confidence on the part of the unions in what management says. Only if it is backed by a manpower planning programme which has already proved itself will an assurance that the long-term effects of a particular policy will be beneficial for employees and not cause redundancies be credible.

The failure of companies to associate manpower planning with industrial relations probably has several causes. Primarily it is the result of a compartmentalised approach to problems: planning is not viewed as a total concept. Just as all consideration of manpower was at one time left out of corporate planning, so when manpower planning is undertaken it is not seen as an all-embracing activity, with industrial relations included in it. On the part of the industrial relations specialist there may also be a lack of understanding that the planning process is flexible and dynamic. Negotiating necessarily means changing and adapting policies, and may therefore seem the antithesis of planning. However, in any sort of real situation, planning must be able to adapt to altered circumstances. The plan that purports to be decided upon, fixed and incapable of being changed, is not worth having.

It may be a part of this lack of understanding of the planning process that results so often in the failure of industrial relations activities to have any coherent, formulated long-term objectives. In many companies, industrial relations is a fire-fighting activity, without any plans of its own. It is not surprising in these circumstances if the connexions between industrial relations and manpower planning are not perceived. But if the company does take the initiative in industrial relations, rather than reacting to events and to union pressures, it will be seen at once that the industrial relations plans are not just relevant to manpower plans: they *are* manpower plans.

MANAGEMENT DEVELOPMENT

Management development has already been referred to under the heading of 'Training' and also as a way of improving utilisation. Its importance is so great in some organisations that it is almost mistaken for manpower planning.

It is often the case that management manpower has a critical importance for a company. All other plans may be dependent on achieving the plans relating to management manpower. A management development programme is both an input to and an output from the manpower plan. The appraisal of individual potential enables management to estimate the future of individuals. This may have organisational implications and thus affect the demand for manpower. It may, on the other hand, indicate a need to recruit 'potential' into the organisation. The past experience of retention of highflyers will be invaluable in arranging the recruitment policy and the way in which such staff are used and developed: this is a straight, manpower planning task. In these senses, management development is an input to the manpower planning process. The validity of the assessments of potential and their value as a factor in estimating the way in which the internal supply will change through promotion is also a possible field for study: a manpower planning/behavioural science problem.

Management development is also an output from the planning process. It is against the background of the overall plan that manpower must be developed. Nothing is worse for the company or for the individual than to develop him in relation to vacancies which are unlikely to occur or which will disappear completely according to current plans. The latter may seem a specially improbable situation, but in companies which fail to keep their personnel manager informed it is not unknown.

Some particular techniques, such as the stationary population model discussed in chapter 4, may be important in the planning of career paths in large organisations. Smaller organisations may adopt the familiar device of replacement charts.

BEHAVIOURAL STUDIES

It will now be clear how most forms of behavioural studies have links with manpower planning or may even be regarded as a part of it. Many studies, for example, have been concerned with labour turnover. Such studies could well be prompted by future difficulties caused by the level of labour turnover; and an assessment of the effect of resultant changes will, in turn, modify forecasts.

Similar considerations apply to other studies. Better selection methods may mean better retention, greater productivity or both. Job rotation and job enrichment programmes have these same connections with manpower planning as well.

Theoretically, organisation development has links with the manpower planning process also. Organisation development—the range of techniques used to develop in individuals a greater awareness of themselves and the effect of their interaction with others—certainly produces changes in individuals; for this is well documented. However, at present the value of these changes for the organisation is less well documented and it is not capable of quantification in any way which will affect a manpower forecast. As knowledge increases, of course, this may cease to be the case.

COST AND BUDGETS

The next step in Fig. 6.1 after examining personnel policies is the assessment of cost. Not only is there the cost of salaries of the manpower and their overheads, but also the cost of the personnel programmes to achieve the manpower supply and the required level of utilisation; and of the training and other personnel policy plans.

These costs must then be considered in the light of overall financial plans. It may be that the financial state of the company is poor: if so, the costs involved may be too great. In this case, therefore, it is necessary to continue around the circle of Fig. 6.1 once more, to re-examine and reassess manpower needs and manpower programmes.

Having reassessed manpower costs it may be possible to accommodate the whole manpower programme within the framework of the company's finances. If not, the arrow pointing upwards indicates that it is the company objectives, or at least their timescale, which must be reassessed.

Once a suitable reconciliation within the financial constraints has been achieved, the manpower plans follow automatically from the 'cycle of decisions'. Indeed, it will be remembered that in chapter 2 the plan was divided into supply, utilisation, training and personnel policies. These are the matters on which the decisions have been taken. In addition there is a forecast of manpower demand, divided into suitable categories.

The interaction with other financial plans is a crucial part of manpower planning. In the case of short-term planning, the financial plans are represented by the budget. Budget and manpower plan are interwoven and must not be thought of as separate entities. The manpower costs will usually be a large, even a major, element in the budget, so that it cannot be compiled without them; yet other costs may affect spending on manpower. The two are, in fact, parts of a single whole, the company's plan. Therefore, they must be compiled in parallel. While it would be logically tidy to plan manpower first and then draw up the budget, it is not normally practical to start planning manpower so long in advance. Starting earlier reduces accuracy, in any case. Furthermore, this system tends to mean that modifications to manpower programmes for financial reasons are not made, because this would entail returning from the budget to an already completed manpower plan. Only organisations not concerned about manpower costs can afford the logically tidy system. Other organisations must develop budgets and manpower plans in parallel.

The interaction of finance and manpower is similar in the long term. In the past, very often financial plans only have been made for long term periods, sometimes even neglecting the manpower results of these plans. Manpower planning can first reveal the implications of financial plans and then develop to the situation where manpower is one of the prime considerations in making the plans.

One organisation, for example, had set financial objectives for marketing in financial terms only, by extrapolation. Manpower plans were made subsequently to check the viability of the forecast. To achieve the financial target, it became clear, firstly, that a considerable increase in sales per man was necessary, and, secondly, that a much larger proportion of the sales force would be junior salesmen, at lower rates of pay. The increase in sales per man had training and management implications, but it hardly required a manpower planner to ascertain this, though it did perhaps require the process of manpower planning to act appropriately on this obvious fact.

The second point, the changed mix of the sales force, while appropriate to the market, had some awkward manpower implications. Junior salesmen already had very high turnover rates, so that the change would put extreme pressure on recruiting and training facilities. It would also make the increased productivity that much harder to achieve. Furthermore, the lower proportion of senior jobs would reduce promotion prospects—hardly a situation conducive to reducing turnover. Only by having a manpower planning system would such problems be brought to light in time to study them and find solutions. In this case the major problem was to find the causes of high turnover.

It will be obvious that a part of the forecast of manpower costs will be affected by future salary and wage administration decisions, so forecasts are necessary. Any fall in the value of money will have an overall effect, but wages and, more particularly salaries, do not merely reflect inflationary pressures. They reflect, to a greater or less degree from company to company, a real rise in the standard of living. It is necessary for the company to be clear about the theoretical basis of its remuneration policies and to be able to assess the effect of them in the future.

MANAGEMENT'S ROLE

Manpower forecasts are not like weather forecasts—forecasts of future events outside the control of the forecaster. Rather, their very purpose is to bring about changes. The forecasts are made so that management can make decisions on the basis of them—and these decisions will result in changing the forecasts themselves: in the jargon, there is 'feed-back' into the forecasting stage of the plan. Indeed, it could be said that the planner has failed if he does not bring about changes that 'invalidate' the forecast which he has made, although it is true that it is a positive decision to decide not to make changes because the forecast manpower situation will be satisfactory.

A. R. Smith [8] has put this point succinctly: Planning should be regarded as a process for providing a frequently updated framework of information for decision-making, with the object of improving the utilisation of resources. . . . It can be argued that, given this philosophy, the organisation which has effective planning procedures can adapt more quickly to new circumstances as they arise.

It is thus clear that it is insufficient for good manpower planning to have a good manpower planner. It is not he who makes the decisions or adapts to new circumstances. It is management. It follows that management must understand the purpose of forecasts. They must also, incidentally, keep the manpower planner informed of their plans; yet managements do fail to involve their personnel specialists in plans for change—an interesting comment in itself on the view taken by them of the value of human resources as well as of their responsibilities towards those whom they employ.

Having provided information on all relevant plans made by them, management cannot even then hand over to the 'black box' of manpower planning [9]. Their part is to use the forecasts as decision-making tools. In an attempt to clarify how they may be used, forecasts can be divided into four types, *most likely, steady state, differential* and *target*. This provides only a rough division of the spectrum of ways of using forecasts and the four types are not even completely distinct from each other, but they do serve to indicate some of the ways of using forecasts.

The most readily understood forecast is one made on a number of assumptions about managerial policy. In effect, the manpower planner predicts management's future decisions, as well as the manpower effects of them, and produces a *most likely* forecast. The important part of the forecast, when it is presented to management, is not just the result of the predictions, but also the assumptions on which they rest. Are they reasonable? How likely are they to turn out to be correct? The next stage is, what action needs to be taken? What will be the effect of this change? The manpower planner must recalculate the forecast on this new basis. All forecasts need constant revision in this way.

If the forecast is not examined like this by management it is being treated as a one-and-only forecast. Its resemblance to this sort of forecast is an inherent danger. For the result often is that what started as an assumption by a relatively junior manpower planner will become the established policy of the company, as manpower forecasts get built into company plans. Forecasts can have this self-realising effect.

This form of *most likely* forecast explores the implications of a certain set of circumstances. A variation of this is to explore the implications of continuing all relevant policies unchanged in the future. This is a most unlikely set of circumstances, but such a *steady-state* forecast can be an important decision-making aid, through pinpointing which policies will cause difficulties and indicating the changes needed. Thus it is more a forecast of what should not happen than of what will. This type of forecast is most developed in the prediction of the effects of promotion policies. It requires management to understand what its purpose is, and this seems to require a length of experience of manpower planning not available in the average company.

Differential forecasts are another method of helping management to decide. Forecasts are made on different sets of assumptions, so that management may decide between them. So many are the possible variations, however, that it is best for management to prescribe the sets of assumptions. This could well be the next stage after thought has been stimulated by a *most likely* or a *steady-state* forecast.

Very similar to the differential forecasting procedure is the *target* forecast. In this, the manpower planner demonstrates the effect of certain management aims, such as reducing the ratio of mates to craftsmen by a given amount. It is best that these targets are suggested or approved by management before incorporation into the overall plan. Otherwise the manpower planner will be tempted to incorporate targets into his *most likely* forecast, because he thinks them worthy and capable of attainment. *Target* forecasts, if approved, require subsequent action to ensure that the targets are attained. The action required is contained in the finally approved *manpower plan*.

It is the function of top management to bring together the work of all in the company into one coherent whole. So, while manpower planning should provide the systems to link together all personnel activities, the board of the company must take the final manpower decisions in the light of all the other areas of concern for the company. In each of these areas, too, plans are needed, so that, in the final analysis, the board can adapt them and weld them into a single corporate plan.

Although it is the board's responsibility to take these decisions, those planning within each function or each division of the company must take cognisance of the fact that there are interactions throughout their plans with other functions in the company. The description of the manpower planning process has indicated how manpower demand forecasts derive from the corporate objectives, how the results of manpower forecasting can provide a feedback into the planning of objectives and how all the manpower decisions feed into and are fed by the financial decisions of the budget. Thus, while final coordinating decisions are the board's, there are many interactions on the way.

The whole context of the objectives of the organisation, which will be incorporated into the marketing plan of the usual company, may also be relevant to manpower planning. The manpower demand forecast is based on the work load envisaged in the corporate plan and, assuming that there is no direct feedback from the manpower plan to the corporate plan, it is entirely derivative. However, there could be factors in the external environment which will affect not only the external supply of manpower but the work which people, internally and externally, will do. The current developments at Volvo and Saab in Sweden to get rid of assembly line work are based on the prediction that Swedes will soon refuse the dull repetition of the assembly line. This is a forecast which is the legitimate province of the manpower planner. It could affect numbers and types of manpower required in the future.

Similarly, internal manpower supply forecasts may be modified from the ordinary extrapolation by the analysis of certain factors in the environment: for example, an increasing acceptance of mothers working, coupled with earlier marriage, smaller families and the provision of nursery schools, could lead to much more stability amongst female labour.

These are some manpower conclusions which might be drawn from a consideration of the manpower environment. In some cases the environment may be considered in relation to manpower only and, for example, Colin Leicester and Judith Hobbs [10] have summarised some of their work in an article which discusses the trends in the distribution of employment between different sectors, in the activity rates of the female population, in the growth of white-collar employment and in the regional distribution of employment.

These factors in the environment are, of course, relevant in other ways to the whole of the corporate plan, affecting the spending patterns of the population, for example, or their aspirations to own certain goods. There are other factors, too, which may have relevance to marketing objectives, manpower plans, or both. There may often be some factual basis for the prediction, such as family expenditure patterns or trends in education, and this whole environment is worth considering for marketing and manpower planning purposes.

A study [11] of this kind, conducted in some depth within Unilever, was published some time ago and it is worth noting here the various broad areas covered. They were: technological changes, psychological changes, social changes (including education), demographic changes (very like the areas discussed by Leicester and Hobbs), industry, economic development, domestic environment, family and social life, personal expenditure. Among the facts examined were:

Energy consumption
Internal passenger transport
Education statistics
Population and birth-rates
Working population
Trade Union membership
Hire purchase debt
House ownership
Consumption of food
Personal consumption

All these factors in the environment may have relevance to the company and should be part of the total corporate planning process. Their relevance has to be assessed by any company, and business strategy worked out in the light of this assessment. There will be uncertainties, but at least all the available, relevant information should be used in making the judgments essential to the task of managing a progressive business. Just as manpower must figure in the corporate plan, so this consideration of the environment should comprehend both manpower and marketing implications.

7

A computer model

The varying sets of assumptions used in the 'differential' and 'target' forecasts are most easily tried out in a computer model. For these types of forecast are merely the substitution of different values for the variables in the forecasting system. Indeed, the 'most likely' and 'steady state' forecasts are just special cases—of a particular set of assumptions. A computer model adds enormously to the range of possibilities which can be tried.

A computer model will itself also be based on a certain set of assumptions, of a slightly different character. This is perhaps best understood by reference to an example of a model. The model described in this chapter is only one of a great many different types of models based on the various forecasting techniques available to manpower planners. This example assumes the use of the *retention profile* as the method of forecasting labour turnover, and thus there is the underlying assumption of length of service as the major determinant of turnover. The model will not prove whether it is the major determinant: it assumes that it is.

Furthermore, it forecasts transfers and promotions in a relatively crude way and there is thus an underlying assumption that turnover is the more important element. These are the assumptions of the model. Yet, within the model one can try out the 'most likely' or any number of differential forecasts of labour turnover patterns, rates of promotion and so on.

Just as any of the forecasting techniques described in the previous chapter on forecasting supply can be used as the basis of a computer program, so models can be built to forecast demand as well. The example in this chapter happens to be concerned with manpower supply and it takes the demand for manpower as 'given'.

The full description of the model which follows may help readers unfamiliar with computer techniques to understand the way in which a forecasting method can be used in a computer model, but readers who do not wish to go to this level of detail may care to skim through the description only before progressing to chapter 8.

RETENTION PROFILE MODEL

This model is based on the retention profile method of analysing wastage. 'Retained staff' are divided each year according to their year of entry (by cohort) and are expressed as a percentage of those who could have left from that cohort in that year. The cohorts are divided by sex and by manpower category within their sex. In calculating the retention profile, the following information about separate year-of-entry cohorts will be required from the computer file in the computer print-out, for each category in each division of the organisation:

1. Length of service at end of year (e.g. under 1 year, 1 year, 2 years, ... 9 years, 10 years).
2. Number of employees at end of year for each length of service division.
3. Normal retirements (at age 65) during year.
4. Leavers excluding normal retirements during year divided into:
   (a) Hard-core (death and other retirements)
   (b) Others.

This division is made because it is relevant to some applications of manpower planning although it does not figure in this forecasting method.

These are tabulated as in Table 7.1 to calculate the retention profiles for each length of service category.

Table 7.1 has not taken into account movements into categories (i.e. from another category within the division), transfers in from another division, movements out of categories and transfers out. We shall want to consider, when forecasting, the overall retention percentages, that is, taking into account wastage, transfers out and movements out of categories, and also the fact that there will be transfers in and movement into categories during the year and that some of these may leave. We shall also want to know the proportion of leavers throughout the year who are transfers out and movements out of categories. We shall then want to consider the number of transfers in and movements into categories during the year as ratios of the number at the beginning of the year.

TABLE 7.1

Category number	Sex	Length of service at end of year 1	Number at end of year 2	Normal retirements 3	Leavers excluding normal retirements Hard-core 4	others 5	Retention percentages after wastage $\dfrac{2}{2+4+5} \times 100$ 6
281	M	Under 1 year	80	2	4	16	80
		1 year	76	1	4	20	76
		2 years	60	3	2	6	88
		3 years	90	4	2	8	90
		—	—	—	—	—	—
		—	—	—	—	—	—
		10 years and over	48	6	3	5	85·8

TABLE 7.2

Category number	Sex	Length of service at end of year	No. at end of year	Retirements	Leavers		Retention after wastage
					Hard Core	Others	
		a_1	b_1	c_1	d_1	e_1	$f_1 = \dfrac{b_1}{b_1 + d_1 + e_1}$
		U.1	b_{10}	c_{10}	d_{10}	e_{10}	f_{10}
		1	b_{11}	c_{11}	d_{11}	e_{11}	f_{11}
		2	b_{12}	c_{12}	d_{12}	e_{12}	f_{12}
		3	b_{13}	c_{13}	d_{13}	e_{13}	f_{13}
		—	—	—	—	—	—
		—	—	—	—	—	—
		—	—	—	—	—	—
		10 years & over	$b_{1,10}$	$c_{1,10}$	$d_{1,10}$	$e_{1,10}$	$f_{1,10}$

The following extra information will, therefore, be required from the computer file for each category within each division:

5. Transfers out during year.
6. Movements out of categories during year.
7. Number of employees at the beginning of years for each length of service division.
8. Transfers in during year.
9. Movements into categories during year.

Table 7.2 shows the information for items 5 and 6 in addition to that already shown in Table 7.1. Table 7.3 completes the information with items 7, 8 and 9.

Explanation of the tables

Table 7.2

Column f_1, the retention after wastage, is the retention profile not taking account of movements between categories and transfers in and out. It is the number at the end of the year as a proportion of the total number who could have left or retired during the year represented as a percentage.

Column i_1, the overall retention, is the number at the end of the

Transfers during year	Movements out of category during year	Overall retention	Proportion of leavers who are transfers out	Proportion of leavers who are movements out of category
	h_1	$i_1 = \dfrac{b_1}{b_1+d_1+e_1+g_1+h_1} \times 100$	$j_1 = \dfrac{g_1}{d_1+e_1+g_1+h_1}$	$k_1 = \dfrac{h_1}{d_1+e_1+g_1+h_1}$
	h_{10}	i_{10}	j_{10}	k_{10}
	h_{11}	i_{11}	j_{11}	k_{11}
	h_{12}	i_{12}	j_{12}	k_{12}
	h_{13}	i_{13}	j_{13}	k_{13}
	—	—	—	—
	—	—	—	—
	—	—	—	—
	$h_{1,10}$	$i_{1,10}$	$j_{1,10}$	$k_{1,10}$

year as a proportion of the total number who could have left, retired moved between categories, or transferred.

j_1 and k_1 are the numbers of transfers out and movements out of categories during the year as proportions of the total numbers who left the category for any reason during the year (i.e. left, moved between categories, transferred or retired).

Table 7.3

e_2 and f_2 are the numbers of movements into categories and transfers in during the year as proportions of the number at the beginning of the year.

Example of tables

An example of these tables is given in Tables 7.4 and 7.5.

The divisions of the company are provided with six-monthly print-outs of some of this information, tabulated on pp. 104 and 105.

COMPARATIVE RETENTION PROFILES

There will be company-wide figures for all the staff generated from the computer file and hence it will be possible to compare the retention

TABLE 7.3

Category number	Sex	Length of service at end of year a_2	Number at beginning of year b_2	Transfers in during year c_2	Movements into category during year d_2	Transfer-in ratio $e_2 = c_2/b_2$	Movements-into-category ratio $f_2 = d_2/b_2$
		U.1	b_{20}	c_{20}	d_{20}	e_{20}	f_{20}
		1	b_{21}	c_{21}	d_{21}	e_{21}	f_{21}
		2	b_{22}	c_{22}	d_{22}	e_{22}	f_{22}
		3	b_{23}	c_{23}	d_{23}	e_{23}	f_{23}
		—	—	—	—	—	—
		—	—	—	—	—	—
		10 years & over	$b_{2,10}$	$c_{2,10}$	$d_{2,10}$	$e_{2,10}$	$f_{2,10}$

N.B. b_{20} = number of starters during the year and not the number of employees at the beginning of the year.

TABLE 7.4   Example based on the pattern shown in Table 7.2

Category number	Sex	a_1	b_1	c_1	d_1	e_1	f_1 %	g_1	h_1	i_1 %	j_1	k_1
281	M	U.1	80	2	4	16	80	2	4	75·44	$\frac{1}{13}$	$\frac{2}{13}$
		1	56	1	4	20	70	4	6	62·22	$\frac{2}{17}$	$\frac{3}{17}$
		2	60	3	2	6	88	2	6	78·9	$\frac{1}{8}$	$\frac{3}{8}$
		3	90	4	2	8	90	4	0	86·5	$\frac{2}{7}$	0
		—	—	—	—	—	—	—	—	—	—	—
		—	—	—	—	—	—	—	—	—	—	—
		—	—	—	—	—	—	—	—	—	—	—
	10 & over	48	6	3	5	85·8	2	2	80	$\frac{1}{6}$	$\frac{1}{6}$

PRINT-OUT 1

| Category number | Sex | Length of service at end of year | Number at end of year | Retirements | Leavers | | Retention after wastage | Overall retention |
					Hard core	Others		

The purpose of this print-out is to examine the morale within the division and to see how the overall profiles compare with the retention profiles after wastage.

As well as printing out the retention profiles for each year of service cohort in each category, it would be interesting to represent them graphically to show how they change between cohorts. This could be done by hand or, preferably, on a graph plotter attached to the computer.

profiles after wastage of similar manpower categories in different divisions or sections. This will give one division (or section of a division) an idea of how it is doing compared with others.

PRINT-OUT 2

Category number	Sex	Length of service at end of year	Number at beginning of year	Number at end of year	Transfers in during year	Transfers out during year	Movements into category during year	Movements out of category during year

This print-out is to examine how promotions and transfers in and out compare with total numbers at the beginning and end of this year.

PRINT-OUT 3

Category number	Sex	Length of service at end of year	Transfer-in ratio	Movement-into category ratio	Proportion of leavers who are transfers-out	Proportion of leavers who are movements of category

Print-outs 1 and 2 will definitely be required by each division every six months, but print-out 3 will not always be required, so there will be provision in the program for an optional print-out of print-out 3.

Although it is not always printed out, print-out 3 could be of interest to the people concerned with doing the calculations.

Print-outs 1, 2 and 3, although prepared every six months, will be rolling annual print-outs.

USE OF RETENTION PROFILE FOR FORECASTING

When considering the progression of the ten cohorts shown in Tables 7.2 and 7.3 over the next three years, we need the following information from the computer file:

TABLE 7.5 Example based on the pattern shown in Table 7.3

Category number	Sex	a_2	b_2	c_2	d_2	e_2	f_2
281	M	Under 1 year	84	4	2	$\frac{1}{21}$	$\frac{1}{42}$
		1 year	60	3	3	$\frac{1}{20}$	$\frac{1}{20}$
		2 years	66	3	11	$\frac{1}{22}$	$\frac{1}{6}$
		3 years	92	2	4	$\frac{1}{46}$	$\frac{1}{23}$
		—	—	—	—	—	—
		—	—	—	—	—	—
		—	—	—	—	—	—
		10 years and over	54	6	3	$\frac{1}{9}$	$\frac{1}{18}$

TABLE 7.6   Year 1 of forecast

Category number	Sex	Length of service a_3	Number at beginning of year b_3	Transfers in during year $c_3 = e_2 \times b_3$	Movements into category during year $d_3 = f_2 \times b_3$	No... retire... dur... ye...
	M/F	Under 1 year	$b_{30} = 100/f_{30} \times R_1$	c_{30}	d_{30}	e_{30}
		1 year	b_{31}	c_{31}	d_{31}	e
		2 years	b_{32}	c_{32}	d_{32}	e
		3 years	b_{33}	c_{33}	d_{33}	e
		—	—	—	—	-
		—	—	—	—	-
		—	—	—	—	-
		10 years & over	$b_{3.10}$	$c_{3.10}$	$d_{3.10}$	e
TOTAL			B_3	C_3	D_3	

$R_1 = \text{Dem}_1 - \sum_{i=1}^{10} S_{1i}$ where $\text{Dem}_1 = $ total manpower demand forecast in the appr... category for year 1

If $b_{30} < 0$, print b_{30}, C_3, D_3, H_3, I_3, and halt program.

TABLE 7.7   Year 2 of forecast

Category number	Sex	Length service a_4	Number at beginning of year b_4	Transfers in during year $c_4 = e_2 \times b_4$	Movements into category during year $d_4 = f_2 \times b_4$	No... retir... dur... ye...
	M/F	Under 1 year	$b_{40} = 100/f_{40} \times R_2$	c_{40}	d_{40}	e_{40}
		1 year	$b_{41} = R_1$	c_{41}	d_{41}	e_{41}
		2 years	$b_{42} = S_{11}$	c_{42}	d_{42}	e
		3 years	$b_{43} = S_{12}$	c_{43}	d_{43}	e
		—	—	—	—	-
		—	—	—	—	-
		—	—	—	—	-
		10 years & over	$b_{4.10} = S_{1.9}$	$c_{4.10}$	$d_{4.10}$	e
TOTAL			B_4	C_4	D_4	

$R_2 = \text{Dem}_2 - \sum_{i=1}^{10} S_{2i}$ where $\text{Dem}_2 = $ total manpower demand forecast in the appr... category for year 2

If $b_{40} < 0$, print b_{40}, C_4, D_4, H_4, I_4, and halt program.

rall file $= i_1$	Number at end of year $g_3 = (b_3 - e_3 + c_3 + d_3)f_3$	Transfers out during year $h_3 = (b_3 - g_3 + c_3 + d_3)j_1$	Movements out of category during year $i_3 = (b_3 - g_3 + c_3 + d_3)k_1$
$= i_{10}$	$g_{30} = R_1$	h_{30}	i_{30}
$= i_{11}$	$g_{31} = S_{11}$	h_{31}	i_{31}
$= i_{12}$	$g_{32} = S_{12}$	h_{32}	i_{32}
$= i_{13}$	$g_{33} = S_{13}$	h_{33}	i_{33}
—	—	—	—
—	—	—	—
$0 = i_{1,10}$	$g_{3,10} = S_{1,10}$	$h_{3,10}$	$i_{3,10}$
	G_3	H_3	I_3

verall rofile $_4 = i_1$	Number at end of year $g_4 = (b_4 - e_4 + c_4 + d_4)f_4$	Transfers out during year $h_4 = (b_4 - g_4 + c_4 + d_4)j_1$	Movements out of category during year $i_4 = (b_4 - g_4 + c_4 + d_4) = k_1$
$= i_{10}$	$g_{40} = R_2$	h_{40}	i_{40}
$= i_{11}$	$g_{41} = S_{21}$	h_{41}	i_{41}
$= i_{12}$	$g_{42} = S_{22}$	h_{42}	i_{42}
$= i_{13}$	$g_{43} = S_{23}$	h_{43}	i_{43}
—	—	—	—
—	—	—	—
$0 = i_{1,10}$	$g_{4,10} = S_{2,10}$	$h_{4,10}$	$i_{4,10}$
	G_4	H_4	I_4

TABLE 7.8 Year 3 of forecast

Category number	Sex	Length of service a_5	Number at beginning of year b_5	Transfers in during year $c_5 = e_2 \times b_5$	Movements into category during year $d_5 = f_2 \times b_5$	No retire dur ye
	M/F	Under 1 year	$b_{50} = 100/f_{50} \times R_3$	c_{50}	d_{50}	e_{50}
		1 year	$b_{51} = R_2$	c_{51}	d_{51}	e_{51}
		2 years	$b_{52} = S_{21}$	c_{52}	d_{52}	e_{52}
		3 years	$b_{53} = S_{22}$	c_{53}	d_{53}	e
		—	—	—	—	—
		—	—	—	—	—
		—	—	—	—	—
		10 years & over	$b_{5,10} = S_{29}$	$c_{5,10}$	$d_{5,10}$	e_5
	TOTAL		B_5	C_5	D_5	E

$R_3 = \text{Dem}_3 - \sum\limits_{i=1}^{10} S_{3i}$ where $\text{Dem}_3 = $ total manpower demand forecast in the appr category for year 3

If $b_{50} < 0$, print b_{50}, C_5, D_5, H_5, I_5, and halt program.

1. Number at the beginning of year 1 of the forecast.
2. Normal retirements in each year of forecast, i.e. numbers reaching retirement age in that year (like the profile, this will be generated by the computer file).

From the information on the computer print-out, and given the numbers at the beginning of year 1 of the forecast for each length of service category, the numbers at the end of the year can be calculated as in Table 7.6.

Explanation of the tables

Column b shows the number at the beginning of the year who can complete the period of service shown in column a during the year, i.e. those shown against '1 year of service' will have completed any length of service *under 1 year*. It follows that those shown against 'Under 1

Overall profile	Number at end of year $$g_5 = (b_5 - e_5 + c_5 + d_5)f_5$$	Transfers out during year $$h_5 = (b_5 - g_5 + c_5 + d_5)j_1$$	Movements out of category during year $$i_5 = (b_5 - g_5 + c_5 + d_5)k_1$$
$= i_1$			
$= i_{10}$	$g_{50} = R_3$	h_{50}	i_{50}
$= i_{11}$	$g_{53} = S_{31}$	h_{51}	i_{51}
$= i_{12}$	$g_{52} = S_{32}$	h_{52}	i_{52}
$= i_{13}$	$g_{53} = S_{33}$	h_{53}	i_{53}
—	—	—	—
—	—	—	—
$0 = i_{1.10}$	$g_{5.10} = S_{3.10}$	$h_{5.10}$	$i_{5.10}$
	G_5	H_5	I_5

year' will not, in fact, have started at the beginning of the year: thus, on line 1, column b holds starters during the year.

As can be seen from Tables 7.6, 7.7 and 7.8, the cohorts move down one line each year, the number at the end of one year being the number for the beginning of the next. The sum of column g as shown above for years 1, 2 and 3 of the forecast (i.e. without new entry 1) is the total internal supply at that date. The difference between this figure and the manpower demand forecast is the additional requirement (i.e. is the figure to appear in column g, line 1). The entry numbers must, however, allow for first year wastage (i.e. the requirement in column g is only i_1 per cent of the entry. For the year 2 forecast (Table 7.7), to supply a cohort with one year's service (i.e. g_{40}), it will be necessary to recruit the number shown at b_{40}.

It is anticipated for forecasting purposes that there will be no new recruits that are likely to retire within three years of joining. This is why some of the entries in columns e_3, e_4, and e_5 have been set to zero.

In forecasting the movements into categories and transfers in, the movements between category and transfer ratios are known (i.e. the numbers of movements between categories and transfers as a proportion of the total number at the beginning of the year) and hence (movement-into-category ratio × number at beginning of year 1 of forecast) gives the number of anticipated movements between categories in year 1 of the forecast, and similarly for transfers. Also the transfers out and movements out of categories as proportions of the total number of leavers during the year are known and hence (movement-out-of-category ratio × total leavers during year 1 of forecast) gives the number of anticipated movements out of category in year 1 of the forecast, and similarly for transfers.

It will be necessary to split each category by sex, because the sexes differ in their retention, and possibly their promotion and transfer, characteristics. To allow the calculation to be made, the manpower demand must be split between the sexes, either on current proportions or through policy decision. However, in many cases the recruitment requirement will be for people, sex being immaterial, so that at the stage at which the first results are being examined, it will be possible to adjust the recruitment numbers for each sex. (Another computer run will be necessary, because of different wastage and other characteristics.)

The footnotes to each table indicate:

(a) That R (recruitment) = Dem (total manpower demand) less $\sum S$ (total internal supply).
(b) That if b_{10} is less than 0, i.e. if the year's recruitment is a negative number, which is equivalent to a forecast of redundancies, the model stops so that consideration can be given to varying transfers or promotions.

Each time these calculations are made (i.e. annually) the following print-outs will be required by each division.

Print-out 4

To find the total transfers in and out and movements between categories in each division for any given year (consider Year 1 of the forecast). The transfers in and out throughout the company should more-or-less balance and this calculation can be made manually. The movements in and out of categories should more-or-less balance within the division.

Category type	Sex	Transfers in	Transfers out	Movements into category	Movements out of category
		G_3	H_3	D_3	I_3

↓
over each
division

TOTAL

Print-out 5

The recruitment figures for three years ahead are also required for each division, so there will be a print-out of the numbers to be recruited in each category for each year of the forecast.

Category type	Sex	Year 1 of forecast	Year 2 of forecast	Year 3 of forecast
		b_{30}	b_{40}	b_{50}

↓
over each
division

TOTAL

Print-out 6

The information overleaf will also be required for inspection by each division for any given year.

How this method of forecasting works is perhaps best illustrated by means of an example given in Tables 7.9, 7.10 and 7.11.

When the calculations of the wastage are made, care must be taken to ensure that the most reliable retention percentages, and movement-between-category and transfer ratios are being used. As time progresses, it will become apparent whether they are changing and in what way, or whether they are remaining steady. Hence, it will be possible to decide which figures to use. The long-term supply forecast resulting from the

PRINT-OUT 6

Category ↓ over each division	Sex	Number at beginning of year B_3	Number at end of year G_3	Wastage $B_3 - G_3 + E_3 + H_3 + I_3$	Retirements E_3
TOTAL					

application of the profile may be amended after a time as more recently obtained information comes to light.

RETIREMENTS

A problem in this method of forecasting arises from retirements. The number of people in any one group who will reach retiring age (i.e. reach age 65) at a certain time is easy enough to calculate, but some of these may die before they are due to retire, and some may retire early due to ill-health, voluntary retirement or early retirement at the employer's request. Early retirement is counted as being a normal 'reason for leaving' (i.e. normal wastage) and is therefore included in the wastage when calculating the retention profile whereas normal retirement is excluded. Since the number of anticipated retirements in any year is subtracted from the number of employees at the beginning of the year, this inclusion will generate errors if no adjustments are made. However, for the present time, the assumption is that the number of employees who retire early for one reason or another is so small that the errors will be negligible.

THE COMPUTER MODEL

This model is concerned only with forecasting manpower supply. The demand forecast is taken as given and input to the model. Models of manpower demand can, of course, be constructed. It is not, in fact, a particularly sophisticated model for supply, but is based on concepts which are fairly readily understood. It places the emphasis on retention

TABLE 7.9   Year 1 of forecast

Category number	Sex	Length of service	Number at beginning of year	Transfers in during year	Movements into category during year	Normal retirements during year	Overall profile %	Number at end of year	Transfers out during year	Movements out of category during year
123	M	Under 1 year	120	5.7	2.85	0	75	90	2.9	5.8
		1 year	100	5	5	0	62	68.2	4.9	7.37
		2 years	88	4	14.6	0	79	84.53	2.75	7.25
		3 years	92	2	4	1	87	84.39	15.61	0
			—	—	—	—	—	—	—	—
			—	—	—	—	—	—	—	—
			—	—	—	—	—	—	—	—
		10 years & over	72	8	9	9	80	64	5.8	5.8
		TOTAL								

If demand = 940, and supply = 850, the requirement at the end of the year for under 1 year's service is 90. This makes the recruitment figure over the course of the year = $100/75 \times 90 = 120$.

TABLE 7.10 Year 2 of forecast

Category number	Sex	Length of service	Number at beginning of year	Transfers in during year	Movements into category during year	Normal retirements during year	Overall profile %	Number at end of year	Transfers out during year	Movements out of category during year
123	M	Under 1 year	133·2	6·34	3·17	0	75	100	3·28	6·56
		1 year	90	4·5	4·5	0	62	62	4·34	6·51
		2 years	68	3·09	11·3	1	79	57·67	3·09	9·27
		3 years	85	1·84	3·68	1	87	77·88	3·6	0
		—	—	—	—	—	—	—	—	—
		—	—	—	—	—	—	—	—	—
		10 years & over	81	—	—	—	—	—	—	—
TOTAL				9	10·2	10	80	72·16	4·67	4·67

If demand = 950, and supply = 850, the requirement at the end of the year for under 1 year's service is 100. This makes the recruitment figure over the course of the year = 100/75 × 100 = 133:2.

TABLE 7.11 Year 3 of forecast

Category number	Sex	Length of service	Number at beginning of year	Transfers in during year	Movements into category during year	Normal retirements during year	Overall profile %	Number at end of year	Transfers out during year	Movements out of category during year
123	M	Under 1 year	120	5·71	2·85	0	75	90	2·96	5·92
		1 year	100	5	5	0	62	68·2	4·90	7·35
		2 years	62	2·8	10·3	0	79	59·33	1·97	5·91
		3 years	58	1·11	2·22	1	87	52·48	8·85	0
			—	—	—	—	—	—	—	—
			—	—	—	—	—	—	—	—
			—	—	—	—	—	—	—	—
		10 years & over	64	7·1	8	9	80	56·08	—	—
		TOTAL								

If demand = 945 and supply = 855, the requirement at the end of the year for 1 year's service is 90. This makes the recruitment figure over the course of the year = $100/75 \times 90 = 120$.

and wastage, rather than transfers and movements between categories. It would, therefore, be unsuitable for an organisation with little turnover but a great deal of internal movement.

The purpose of the example is not to recommend this particular method, but to show how any method can be developed into a forecasting model.

8

Data collection

Lack of data is the most frequent impediment to manpower planning. A prime task of the manpower planner is, therefore, to set up a system for data collection. Unfortunately, data takes time to collect and a system set up now may not be useful for a number of years. Furthermore, a system which has no apparent use when it is first set up, because the information will take time to accumulate, is doomed to failure. Because of these paradoxical constraints, it is usually best to begin manpower planning in some rudimentary form and improve it gradually, using the data from a recording system set up at the same time. It may be possible to gather at least some of the data to make a start from existing records.

If personnel records are inadequate, they may perhaps be supplemented by payroll records. One can usually be sure that the salaries are right, and probably the cost centre numbers, in payroll records. It is often said also that the pension fund records will be extremely reliable, though they may not bother about department or job: they will, however, be absolutely reliable about leavers and can be used for wastage analyses, unless a large proportion of staff are not in the pension scheme or there is a long qualifying period.

The great disadvantage of these records is usually that they are not designed for statistical analyses. Even records about leaving are frequently difficult to analyse. The detail is either in a book or on the old record card. The book will be in chronological order; the cards probably in alphabetical order, in years if the manpower planner is lucky. After all, the personnel department only keep them so that they can give references! The analysis of data in this form usually requires a long and dull 'manual' exercise.

Figure 8.1 shows a form which might be used to analyse labour turnover. A separate sheet is used for each leaver. The sheets can then be sorted according to department, according to type of employee and according to reason for leaving. The sheet, incidentally, shows one possible way of classifying reasons for leaving. A similar form (Fig. 8.2) can be used for age and length of service analysis. Although such analyses do not provide a very precise way of determining what is likely to happen, they may provide some indications of impending problems. If no other information is available this may be useful.

Meanwhile, the more complete data system is being set up and at least the bulk of the information should be of immediate use. Luckily the personnel data needed for manpower planning does not differ significantly from data generally needed for the more traditional forms of personnel management. The difference lies in the analysis. Therefore it will usually be the case that virtually no new items of data will appear in the system. However, the system will retain history, so that analyses can be made, and organise the recording to facilitate this.

Naturally, analysis of data is easier in a computerised system, but a smaller firm may decide that a reorganisation of its manual system is all that can be justified economically. It is important to realise that manpower planning is not dependent on having a computer. This chapter is written in the context of a computerised scheme, but much of it can be applied to a manual system using ordinary record cards or punched cards.

It is worth pointing out also that there is a good deal of data required for effective manpower planning which is not obtainable from personnel records, computerised or not.

Firstly, there is all the production data required for many forms of manpower demand forecasting. It is necessary for the planner to ensure that this is kept (it usually is) and that it is subdivided suitably for an investigation of appropriate demand forecasting techniques (it often is not). Obviously, production data must relate to recognisable manpower groupings.

Secondly, forgotten organisation changes can play havoc with an analysis of data. The personnel manager may remember that thirty men were transferred to the main production unit when the new product went into full production after an experimental period, but not if he joined the company only last year. And personnel records will reveal the information only with intensive analysis, especially if twenty-eight of the men have left and their records are now filed as leavers—alphabetically and in the basement. It is useful, therefore, to maintain a record of organisational changes and their manpower and production implications.

TURNOVER—SPECIAL ANALYSIS

Monthly	
Office Weekly	✓
Factory Weekly	

Female [ ]
Leave blank if male

Reasons for leaving code
↓

Department		Code		Reason
MD		01		Remuneration/condition
Manufacturing—A		02		To further career
Manufacturing—B		03		Location
QC	✓	04		Dissatisfied—job
Central Control		05		—working conditions
U.K. Marketing—HQ		06		—supervision
U.K. Marketing—Field		07		—colleagues
Surgical		08		—hours
Marketing Res.		09		Resigned after warning
Personnel		11		Marriage—to rejoin
Medical		12		—not to rejoin
Finance		13		Pregnancy
Management Serv.		14		Domestic responsibility
Purchasing		15		Moving
Export		16	✓	Emigrating
Continental		17		Giving up work
Corporate		18		Resig.—health
Int. Marketing		19		Further education
Research		20		Other/N.K.
Development		30		Left w/o notice
		41		Dismissed—ill health
		42		—unsuitable
		43		—misconduct
		44		—failed medical
		51		Redundancy—voluntary
		52		—enforced
		61		Retirement—ill health
		62		—early, voluntary
		63		—early, enforced
		64		—at normal age
		70		Death
		80		End of temp. engagement

FIG. 8.1   Manual analysis of labour turnover

SPECIAL ANALYSIS

AGE at 1.1.69

1/04 − 12/08		60/64
1/09 − 12/13		55/59
1/14 − 12/18		50/54
1/19 − 12/23		45/49
1/24 − 12/28		40/44
1/29 − 12/33		35/39
1/34 − 12/38		30/34
1/39 − 12/43		25/29
1/44 − 12/47		21/24
1/48 ⟶		U.21

SERVICE at 1.1.69

⟶ 12/28		40+
1/29 − 12/33		35/39
1/34 − 12/38		30/34
1/39 − 12/43		25/29
1/44 − 12/48		20/24
1/49 − 12/53		15/19
1/54 − 12/58		10/14
1/59 − 12/63		5/9
1/64 − 12/67		1/4
1/68 ⟶		U.1

FIG. 8.2   Manual analysis of age and service. Note: Dates run forwards because this is the way in which one most easily recognises dates

SETTING UP A PERSONNEL DATA SYSTEM

It has already been implied that the data base for manpower planning should be the personnel record system. It is, however, an advantage of a computerised system that a sub-system of the data required for manpower planning can then be obtained by computer means if the whole personnel file is unnecessarily large for processing for the purpose of manpower planning.

It will probably also be a sensible course to combine with payroll. This not only gives the system the impetus needed to keep it up-to-date and the priority accorded to paying staff, but also avoids an unnecessary duplication. In some circumstances, manpower needs can be built on to an existing payroll system, but this can lead to an unsatisfactory compromise.

This is not the place to give detailed consideration to setting up a computerised personnel information system: Edgar Wille [1], Joan Springall [2] and the O.E.C.D [3], go into further detail on this. However, it is necessary to examine the overall process of setting up a data file and to look in more detail at some of the manpower planning needs.

The first step in setting up a system is to examine existing demand for data—and here 'demand' may well be less than 'need', just as it may be with manpower demand. This is conveniently done as a matrix of 'outputs' from the existing system compared with the data elements required for it. Table 8.1 is an example.

The next step is to examine each output to see if it is really needed and, if it is, whether it would be better in some other form. It may be

TABLE 8.1   Analysis of present returns and records before computerisation

	Manual record card	Strength return	Part-time employees return	Salary review sheets	Labour turnover return	Appraisal forms	RDP return	Compa-ratios	Holiday entitlement lists
Existence of 'live' record		✓	✓		✓		✓	✓	✓
Name/initials	✓			✓		✓			✓
Mr/Mrs/Miss	✓			✓		✓			
Sex	✓	✓	✓		✓				
Address	✓								
Date of birth	✓			✓		✓			
Date engaged	✓			✓		✓			✓
N.I. no.	✓								
Marital status	✓								
Children	✓								
Pension fund member	✓								
Notice period	✓								
Job title: present	✓	✓		✓		✓			
history	✓								
Job title dates	✓					✓			
Qualifications	✓							✓	
Salary: present	✓			✓					
history	✓			✓					
Salary dates	✓			✓					
Resignation date	✓				✓				
Reason for leaving	✓				✓				
Co./Dept./Branch	✓	✓	✓		✓	✓		✓	✓
Cost centre no.	✓			✓					
Grade	✓			✓		✓		✓	✓
Normal hours	✓		✓	✓					✓
Holiday entitlement								✓	
RDP	✓								
Appraisal code				✓		✓		✓	
Salary ranges									
Establishment		✓							
Past strengths					✓				

that the analysis is constrained by the limitations of the existing data system or by the sheer work involved in a better analysis. For example, labour turnover may be expressed using the BIM formula, not because a better measure is not preferred, but because other measures are more difficult to compile.

The third step is to consider other outputs which might be useful and at this point manpower planning comes in. What are the manpower planning outputs?

TABLE 8.2   Outputs from computer file

1.   Employee profile and change notice
2a. Salary planning sheets
2b. Salary plan reminders
2c. Staff notification
3a. Appraisal forms
3b. Appraisal analysis
4.   Manpower planning:
    4a. Retention profile
    4b. Strength return: compares with budget
    4c. Labour turnover index
    4d. Age distribution—various parameters
    4e. Length of service distribution—various parameters
    4f. Cohort analysis
5.   Salary administration:
    5a. Compa-ratios
    5b. Average earnings
6.   General retrieval

Table 8.2 shows the outputs listed in a feasibility study for a computerised system at United Dominions Trust Ltd. It includes the initial manpower planning requirements. Output 1 is the replacement for the personnel record card, which is often usefully combined or linked with the document by which changes are input to the computer. This will bear all the information held (or, at least, most of it) about an individual. The outputs numbered 2 are concerned with reviewing salaries (2a), reminding managers of planned reviews (2b) and producing a letter to staff telling them of the review (2c); 3a and 3b are the appraisal forms and the analysis of results of appraisals.

The manpower planning outputs are in the main self-explanatory. Output 4b is a strength return (by departments) in which the strength is compared with the manpower budget. How this can be done is discussed below. Naturally, various parameters can be set for most of these returns, giving the turnover by department, by grade or by particular categories of manpower. In the case of length of service, service with the Company is the normal measure, but length of service in a particular grade may be needed in studies of promotion paths (and is needed in salary administration).

Output 5a is the ratio of average salary in the grade to the grade mid-point. Output 6 is not really an output, but a means of obtaining outputs. A general retrieval program (there is usually one available for the computer in use) enables simpler analyses to be done on demand. Normally, the high level language used enables a member of the personnel department, after some training, to formulate these enquiries himself. This program will deal with such queries as: 'How many staff were there in Department X on such-and-such a date?' It would also allow the analysis of reasons for leaving, this being a particularly simple form of analysis.

These outputs can be checked against the matrix and any new data items required entered. The final step is then to consider if there are other items which seem to have a potential use for analytical purposes. The temptation to enter items unlikely to be used for a long time should be avoided: they will not be kept up-to-date.

Data items should be judged primarily by the part they play in analyses needed or likely to be needed. Other items may be necessary if searches are to be conducted. For example, birth date is needed for age analyses, amongst other things. Ability to speak Russian, however, may never be analysed, but a search may be needed when a letter from Russia is received and needs to be translated. Finally, some items may be included so that the employee profile is complete, e.g. address. However, there may be individual details where it is better to look at the individual's files, for, even if manual record cards have gone, personal files will remain. An example might be next of kin.

The data elements can then be listed, as in Table 8.3. This is a list of data elements for the personnel file only of a linked personnel file and payroll file system: payroll data, therefore, does not appear. It is, of course, only one possible list. Other companies may have other needs: languages spoken may be important, for example. It does, however, indicate the type of listing needed.

The final step in deciding on the contents of the computer file, after reviewing the data elements on each employee by the method described, is to consider all other items of information which might be held about individuals. These items should be considered in the light of possible analyses and thus of their potential usefulness. However, they should be included in the file sparingly and with caution. Clearly, there is no immediate use for them and data items which are unused provide no

TABLE 8.3 Contents of personnel file

	Contents	*Notes*
Identity	Personnel number	
Personal	Surname—first name—	
Details	initials	
	Address	
	Postal code	Postal code can be used for sorting, e.g. analysing travel arrangements, planning changes in location.
	Date of birth	
	Sex	
	Marital status	
	Date of marriage ⎫	Pension scheme purposes.
	Maiden name ⎭	Also, difficulties can occur in tracing individuals who join with one name, marry and leave with another.
	Alien/Non-alien/EEC alien	Because aliens require work permits.
	Immigrant/Non-immigrant ⎫	For analysis of success of
	Colour ⎭	good race relations policy.[4]
Joining	Date of joining	
	Calculated date	A notional date to give correct length of service if service is broken.
	Recruit source	Whether from university, school, same or different industry, etc.
	Recruit method	Whether through advertising, agencies, etc. (This is not a complete way of analysing advertising because it does not have information about response, quality of other candidates etc.)
Job	Job title	Uncoded, in plain language for print-out.
	Occupation code	Occupation codes are discussed subsequently in the chapter.
	Date of change of code	For analysis of promotion.

TABLE 8.3 *continued*

	Contents	Notes
Location	Company—Sub-code	Department, in effect. This is designed for a Company with subsidiaries.
	Cost centre— Date	Date is important for analysis of internal transfers.
	Cost centre of manager's manager	See Note 2 below.
	Location code	Actual building.
	Personnel office	Code of appropriate personnel office, to whom employee profile will be sent.
Salary	Current salary	
	Grade	Computer might also hold ranges which are applied to grade: if held separately, range changes can be effected easily.
	Grade location variation	Different ranges used in different areas: others may have separate London allowance.
	Date of change	Date when salary and/or grade last changed.
	Reason for change	e.g. merit review, general increase, re-grading, etc.
	Planned salary increase 1 ⎫ Planned date 1 ⎬ Planned salary increase 2 ⎭ Planned date 2	Computer can then calculate cost of plans and generate reminders.
Performance	Last appraisal result Date of appraisal Date of next appraisal Potential rating	
Conditions	Hours ⎫ Holiday entitlement ⎬ Period of notice ⎭	Mainly for employee profile's completeness.
Indicators	Eligible for overtime	Overtime rates held on payroll file.
	Shift allowance	Amount held on payroll file.
	Company car Company mortgage On day release Registered disabled person	
Pension	Eligibility	
	Scheme	Necessary if several schemes operate.
	Entry date	If different from date of joining.
	Retirement date	(More information may be needed in some schemes.)

TABLE 8.3 *continued*

	Contents	Notes
Leaving	Reason for leaving	
	Date	
Education	Level	Broad indication, e.g. graduate, O levels, etc.
	Field	Broad indication of field of specialist education.
Professional Qualifications	Field	Similar broad qualifications.
	Description	Actual initials for print-out: e.g. ACCA.
Training	Date of course	
	Int./Ext.	Company course or outside.
	Course code/Field	Actual course (coded) if internal or indication of field of study if external.
	Description	Optional field for external courses.
	Length of course	
History	Date of change	(History is discussed subsequently in the chapter.)
	Type of change	e.g. salary, grade or job.
	Salary	
	Grade	
	Appraisal code	
	Potential rating	
	Reason for change	
	Occupation code	
	Job title	Included so that personal history is easily read.
	Cost centre	

Notes

1. Absence records are not included, because they have a direct effect on payroll and form part of that file (National Insurance contributions are affected). In fact, a full record of absence, e.g. dates of absence, to give length of absences and total days lost, can use a great deal of file space. Some simplified record, e.g. number of absences and total days lost, may suffice.

2. A relatively minor problem is that heads of cost centres are, on some costing systems, included in the cost centre; in others, they are included in their manager's cost centre. In either case, in some analyses, the other system will be more appropriate. In this file they are included in their own cost centres, so that the salary cost of a department is easily calculated. However, for salary review purposes, they must be excluded; otherwise, they will be reviewing their own salaries. The inclusion of their managers' cost centre numbers enables the computer to exclude them from their own review sheets and to include them on those of their managers.

incentive for keeping them up to date. There is a danger, then, if the file is not wholly up-to-date, that it will fall into disrepute and adversely affect that part which is being used. It is usually better not to try to be wholly comprehensive, but to organise the file in such a way that additions can be made to it.

It will be clear that this data file content provides all the information for the outputs listed in Table 8.2, that is, for all the personnel requirements, including manpower planning. In fact, manpower planning does not require special personnel data. Since it coordinates all the normal personnel activities, it requires only the same data. However, it does require that these data are more readily analysable than is usual, and the computer file must be organised accordingly. In addition, past data must be analysable and, in order to make analysis possible, suitable coding must be devised. These three areas—file organisation, historical data and coding—are, therefore, worth exploring in the context of manpower planning.

FILE ORGANISATION

The manpower planning requirements, especially at the corporate level in a large organisation, will not cover all the data items discussed above. Nevertheless, the data file containing all the items can be used for the analyses. It may be more convenient, however, to have a separate file of only those data elements required, particularly if the full records are held in a number of separate files for different divisions or if the system is so large and well used that access for manpower planning analyses may be difficult at times.

For many analyses, it is not necessary to be absolutely up-to-date. Indeed, much of the analysis will be of data on past strengths, leaving rates, promotion probabilities and so on. Therefore, a sub-file for manpower planning can be 'stripped off' the main file or files at intervals and then used for analyses. The main file would, of course, still have to be used for monitoring strengths but all analysis could be transferred to this sub-file. Table 8.4 lists a possible file content for such a file.

Personnel and payroll link

The possibility of building the personnel file on to a payroll system has already been mentioned. In any case, it is strongly recommended that the two systems be combined in some way. Much of the information

TABLE 8.4 Manpower planning sub-file

Contents	Notes
Number	Name is not necessary in analyses
Sex	
Date of birth	
Date of joining company	
Date of leaving company	
Reason for leaving	
Qualifications	It may be desirable to analyse the performance of different types of staff.
Appraisal and potential ratings	These may also be useful in analysing prospects.
Departments	Past, present and dates.
Job codes	Past, present and dates.
Salary*	Past, present and dates
Grade	Past, present and dates.

* Salary may not be very useful, although it is likely to be accurate: if past history is to be put on the computer when the file is set up it may be the only accurate indication of past changes.

is common to both systems and there is unnecessary duplication of input if there are two systems. Even if common input documentation is used, the separation of the two is unsatisfactory. They are likely to drift apart and much time can be spent, really rather fruitlessly, in reconciling the two.

There may even be political advantages in combining the two. Often the payroll is not a Personnel Department responsibility and coordination of the two records systems for payroll and personnel is made more difficult. If both departments use one system—on the impersonal computer—their coordination can, in fact, be enhanced. Furthermore, the payroll must be accurate. In a combined system this need for accuracy can pervade the personnel elements also.

It is possible to combine the two systems totally, so that an individual record contains all the personnel data and payroll data (tax code, tax paid to date, deductions for National Insurance, overtime worked, etc.). However, since payroll is a regular requirement, and its compilation does not require any of the other data, two linked files—linked by computer means—may be a suitable answer.

Figure 8.3 shows how this method might work. Updating would be by computer means, so that a change of salary in one file would automatically adjust the other. However, in the main there is no duplication of data, only personnel number, name, basic salary and cost code being on both files. Outputs, as shown, would sometimes come from one file, sometimes from the other and occasionally from both files run together.

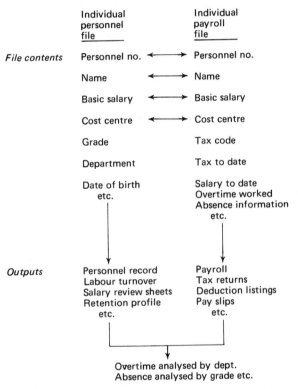

FIG. 8.3   File organisation: 1. *Linked personnel and payroll files*

Individual or characteristic organisation

It perhaps should be mentioned that there are two ways of organising the data in the personnel file itself. The usual system is for the information about one individual to follow consecutively on the disc or tape. The meaning of each item is often dependent on its position in the series, e.g. the third item under each individual will be his grade, but this is not essential and other computer methods of identification can be adopted. A mixed system may be suitable: for example, the first items will be identified by position, which necessitates the fields being of fixed length, but the later items, such as training undergone and history, need to be of variable length and are identified by other means.

However, it is possible to organise the file by characteristics, so that under Grade 1 all in that grade are listed, under Grade 2 all in that grade are listed and so on. This system is obviously advantageous if simple listings are a frequent requirement and might possibly be considered for a system used basically for short-listing candidates, but is not particularly helpful in most cases. It will be readily appreciated that the production of the employee profile is actually hampered by the system, since the details of an individual are scattered throughout the file.

Therefore, the usual system of organisation by individual is normally adopted in preference to organisation by characteristics.

Individual and job files

For the manpower planner and for the personnel manager with manpower control responsibilities, details of individuals are only part of the data. The other side of the coin is the jobs they occupy and, possibly, the jobs that exist (or are authorised) but happen not to be filled at the moment. One way of dealing with this is to have two interlinked files. One would be a personnel file of the type discussed already, containing a record for each employee, and the other a jobs file, containing a record for each post authorised, whether it is filled or not.

Figure 8.4 shows these two files and their uses.

The individual file produces all the outputs discussed already. In combination, it is possible to compare the numbers of staff in different categories with the plan, or budget, for the year and thus produce various forms of manpower monitoring report. It would also be possible to list vacancies at any given time.

By itself, the job file, with a suitable job numbering system, could produce organisation charts—and, in combination with the personnel file, show the names of the posts' occupants. It might also be used for costing, especially if certain posts are costed on a predetermined system to various functions. Thus, if the post has two different occupants on different salaries in one year and a period of vacancy between, the job file would accumulate the correct amounts for allocation to the functions concerned.

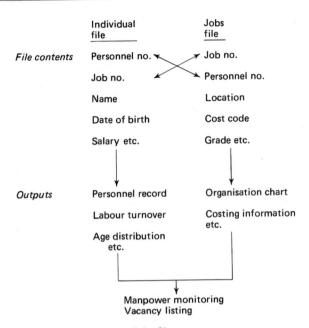

FIG. 8.4   File organisation: 2. *Jobs file*

The system also allows the sophistication of a post graded at one level being occupied by someone who is personally on a different grade. However, it is usually not necessary to keep the system quite this pure and the personal grade in the ordinary personnel file will usually suffice, with an indication that it is a personal grade. It is even possible to produce the monitoring reports without two files: if the planned manpower is held for the year on a set of punch cards or a tape, it can be fed into the computer each month for comparison with the actual strength.

Thus, this elaboration of the system, whilst useful, particularly in a large organisation, is not essential to a computerised personnel information system.

HISTORICAL DATA

Most manpower planning methods consist of an analysis in one form or another of what has happened in the past. Historical data is therefore essential on a computer file. Nevertheless certain decisions have to be made about what historical information to keep and for how long.

The data file given as an example in Table 8.3 suggested the items needed. Grade changes and occupation code changes are needed to analyse promotion (and salary history may be used for similar purposes). Departmental codes (cost centre in the example) are needed to analyse transfers. Appraisal and potential ratings are included so that their value (or lack of value) as predictions can be established. In addition, of course, the records of leavers must be retained, with their histories, so that a full analysis of the past staffing can be made, and so that wastage can be analysed. This information must extend back over a reasonably long period of time: it is obviously not sufficient merely to keep the last two or three changes. It is simplest to keep all history, and this may be the best method. One is then sure that everything that can be required is there. But this may seem a little extravagant.

If a limitation is to be placed on the historic data, it is clearly least complicated to keep a given number of changes. This leads to the unsatisfactory situation of having a short history of the man who has risen quickly through a number of jobs and a long history for others. It is therefore suggested that a time limit, though more complicated to operate since it necessitates fields of variable lengths, is necessary.

The time limit will vary according to the changeability of the company, but five years seems suitable in many cases. The validity of forecasts based on analyses going back beyond five years seems likely to be in doubt in all but the most stable conditions.

A final decision is whether at 'initial loading' to include all history. Whether this is possible at all will depend on the state of the manual records: it has already been suggested that only salary may be fully reliable. Furthermore, unless leavers in the past are also included, this history will not be helpful for the majority of analyses, and the records of leavers may be much more difficult to 'load'. Without them the advantage is a complete record print-out, but the cost for this small gain is high.

In many cases a compromise may seem the best course. The history of the last year would enable immediate retention analyses to be made and would help at once in salary administration uses. As soon as the system is running, it begins to generate its history from that point onwards. It may be more important to get the system running for the more mundane uses before attempting the sophisticated analyses. It may be there will be sufficient problems to sort out even so! But the morale of the users and the DP staff will be enhanced if the system begins to prove useful as soon as possible and a start is not delayed by the mammoth task of coding data and entering it on the file.

CODING

A number of the items of data will need coding. Figure 8.1 which shows a means of collecting data manually also, incidentally, shows a coding system for reasons for leaving. The two digit system illustrates the 'hierarchical' classification of reasons, which can aid some analyses, so that one can classify reasons meaningfully into 'Avoidable resignation' (Codes 01–09), 'Unavoidable resignation' (Codes 11–19), all dismissals (Codes 41–44) and so on.

Other data items need coding. The most crucial coding problem is that of occupational classification. It has been continually emphasised that a frequent impediment to manpower planning is lack of data. In setting up an occupational classification one is providing the source of data for manpower planning in the future. It is, therefore, important that the classification will be useful for manpower planning in the future; for it will be too late to alter it then.

But it is not only important to get it right, it is also difficult. In the first place, because its major usefulness is not now but in the future, it may be difficult to get resources and attention devoted to it. In the second place, although many may at first sight think it is easy to classify manpower in their company, it becomes more difficult as one thinks through the task, because manpower needs to be classified in different ways for different purposes.

It may, for example, help a managing director to note trends and thus to control manpower to watch the changes in numbers of skilled, semiskilled and unskilled men in a factory. A forecast in these terms might give some indication to the recruitment manager of the sort of recruits he will need: x apprentices, y trained craftsmen, z entrants to the operator training school and so on. But will he not then need to know which craft: how many fitters, how many electricians? And then he needs to think of the intakes: some are school-leavers, but he needs school-leavers for office jobs also.

We might then turn to management and supervisory training, or organisational matters like the span of control. We need to know how many managers and how many supervisors; so we need classifications to distinguish them. But might we not now want to classify the electricians' foreman as a supervisor, when in assessing future craft training needs we wanted to classify him as an electrician?

If the answer is 'yes', we need a multi-axial, or at least a bi-axial, system. In such a system there is a code in which each digit or groups of digits represents a different aspect of the job and can be arrived at more or less independently. They can be used separately for analyses or in combination. This is a firm conclusion. There are possibly also two rather more tentative conclusions. First, the discussion has been related to the type of manpower required and to the training needs: it is suggested that it is in this sort of dimension in which one should think, rather than (for example) in the dimension of company organisation. In any case, the organisation is more liable to unpredicted and sudden change, and the manpower data will, no doubt, include information about division and department. Even so, it may not be easy to group staff according to main training needs. It may be clear that the engineers as a group are of engineering degree level, the technicians form another main group, even the administrators form some sort of cohesive group, needing a professional qualification or equivalent experience. Many engineers become salesmen and do the same job as arts graduates and quite unqualified men. Is the need to group all salesmen together? Or is it better to group all engineering graduates together? A multi-axial system means that the two elements need not be lost—it will still be possible to have an education digit or a separate field for this—but it may be convenient in overall classifications to have a main group of salesmen, rather than a main group of graduate engineers.

Second, the needs of the particular company in using manpower data have sprung to mind in considering classification. It is probable that the occupation classification must be specific to the organisation. At present, in any case, there is no standardised system which a company can adopt: it may be that there will not be. A national system must cope with all sorts of occupations which the company does not have and must, therefore, have elements which the company does not need: it is important, if the code is to be properly used, that it be as easy to use as possible and that it seem to be relevant. Furthermore, it is easy for a national system to fail to make distinctions which are needed by the company.

This is not to say that it is not useful to look at national systems and, if they are adopted for national statistics, to ensure that one's own classification system will allow statistics to be compiled for this system. Certainly until national systems are fixed, one may have to be content with an assessment that the company system provides at least as fine a breakdown of the work force as the Government will ask for. If the systems then are not compatible, the computer will still be able to provide the statistics with the help of a 'look-up table', held on the computer.

A fuller treatment of occupational classification is given elsewhere [5], but it is worth looking here briefly at current systems, because, even if they cannot be used directly and unchanged, their concepts may be adopted.

The Department of Employment's system, for their own use, is known as CODOT and they also have a key list of about 400 job titles. This is, in fact, a list of job titles, each with a code. In other words, it is single-axis and the codes are not arranged in a way which lends itself to computer analysis.

The Department of Trade and Industry system has five axes:

1. Sphere or objective
2. Function
3. Job authority
4. Job skill
5. Level of job skill

Thus, returning to the example of supervisor and craftsmen, this code would be able to distinguish the supervisory content on axis 3 and the skill on axes 4 and 5. Actually, the system, being constructed for national purposes and for dealing with technological and scientific manpower, would not distinguish specifically a craft level, but in principle it could. Similarly, the Sphere axis (e.g. Defence, Nuclear) is more likely to be useful at national level: often the whole company will have the same code.

The Institute of Manpower Studies System (IMSSOC) is similar in concept. Its axes are:

1. Job activity
2. Job activity level
3. Job authority level
4. Job knowledge

Within these axes, the hierarchical approach can be adopted, so that the first digit of job activity can give main groups, and a more detailed breakdown within those groups in the second and so on until the job title is reached.

It will be clear that axis 1, with axis 2 and axis 3 are the dimensions needed to deal with the supervisor craftsman. It will be clear also that the hierarchy within axis 1 can vary from company to company, so that the system is adapted to the particular needs of the company.

9

Manpower controls

The orthodox view of personnel management only a few years ago was that it was a service function. It acted, the view ran, as a service to, and at the behest of, line management. It recruited suitably, as required by line management; it trained suitably; it supplied information about manpower on which line management might (or, more likely, might not) act.

This was an oversimplified picture. It was perhaps a reaction to the earlier welfare orientation of personnel management: it was a way of emphasising that personnel management was concerned with the same broad objectives as line management—the objectives of the company.

Another 'service' provided to management was advice on matters concerned with manpower. Advice to managers down the line fits in with this picture. Advice to top management begins to break it down. What, for example, if the personnel manager advises, for the sake of future management needs, that some graduate engineers be recruited? The line manager may well, for understandable reasons, prefer ex-apprentices who have slightly lower academic qualifications but who have experience of the work to be undertaken: he, after all, is controlled by his achievement of this year's targets and cannot afford to take an idealistic view of long-term future requirements. If the board accepts the personnel manager's advice, however, he must accept it also. The board may then charge the personnel manager with recruiting and placing the graduates: the advisory role, once the decision is taken by the board, becomes in the true sense an executive role. The transition from advice to executing the tasks advised requires only board approval and, as manpower questions are better analysed and manpower decisions are taken more consciously and more rationally by management, so the transition happens more frequently. As well as delegating the execution, the board may even delegate some of the decisions, although, if it is wise it will have set the framework. The interaction of the different plans and thus of different specialists does not allow total delegation: the basic planning decisions are the prime role of top management.

It would not be surprising, therefore, if the control of manpower, within the overall manpower plan, were delegated to the manpower planners. This task, while logical enough, has a number of inherent problems, which need to be examined.

The distinction was made in chapter 2 between long-range and short-range manpower planning. In dealing with control problems we are naturally dealing with short-range forecasts. Planning is a dynamic process and, therefore, one never actually 'gets to' the current long-range forecasts. (This is not to say that one cannot check the early long-range forecasts against what actually happens. The analysis of the reasons for the forecasts being wrong can help with future forecasting.) The short-range manpower forecast and plans, therefore, are also the basis of the manpower control system, and these are inextricably mixed up with the financial budget. Some of the problems of manpower control are merely images of the problems of budgeting; others are particular to manpower.

Before examining these problems, it is worth considering why there should be any manpower controls at all. There is a school of thought which says that it is sufficient to give a manager—indeed, better to give a manager—a financial budget only and then let him spend it. In its extreme form this view precludes any manpower planning at all. It is, however, possible to recognise the need to make manpower plans, for the sake of efficient recruitment and training, but then not to use them as controls. The difficulty of this is that it is that much more difficult to get the manpower planning exercise taken seriously if there is no monitoring subsequently. This is the first reason for monitoring the manpower plans: the practical reason that it requires that plans are made conscientiously. The other reasons are of motivation, of long-term effect, of adaptability, and of social responsibility.

The setting of targets is a compromise between complete control of a situation, which allows no scope for the manager to act on his own initiative, and the failure to set even any guidelines, so that the manager is unable to decide for himself what is the right course of action in a given situation. Both extremes remove freedom of action, and thus initiative: in both cases, the manager has to defer to his superiors on even minor matters if his actions are to be a proper part of the company's plan. Therefore, the middle course of targets in major areas would seem to be necessary to motivate the manager properly and allow him sensibly to use his initiative. For this reason, manpower plans are needed.

Furthermore, the budget is a short-term matter. Manpower decisions have long-term effects. Many courses of action may cost much the same now, and thus be allowable on the basis of the financial budget, but have very different future effects. A recruitment embargo now can lead to a lack of managers in ten years' time. A cutback in apprentices means fewer craftsmen in five years' time. A recruitment drive at the end of the year may cost little this year, but have a heavy cost in salaries throughout next year. Even the short-term decisions on manpower must be taken in the context of their long-term effects. Some guidelines for manpower decisions are necessary.

Guidelines are not rigid controls. It has already been argued that planning allows adaptability because it provides a thought-out base from which to depart. As well as adaptability, the manpower plan ensures that the people concerned, the employees, are regarded as people and not just something on which money is spent. It is the social responsibility of the company to do this.

THE ESTABLISHMENT VIEW

A major problem in the use of budgetary controls, financial or manpower, is the need to prevent managers, at board level as well as below, from thinking of the budget as an upper limit. If they do this, all sorts of awkward consequences follow. In manpower terms, this is thinking of the manpower forecast as an *establishment* [1]. Once thinking is in those terms, it follows that the establishment will not represent a forecast of what is expected to happen. If it is the upper limit, then at least in some areas it will not be reached. The total establishment will be a higher number than actual manpower is likely to reach, indeed than anyone expects it to reach.

It is difficult, and not without danger, to consider a failure to come up to budget as worthy of investigation as an over-budget position. But if the budgeting is to be given an accurate picture of future needs this must be done. The danger, of course, is that the manager will use manpower up to the permitted level even if this is unnecessary. There is a need here for a measure of confidence between the manager and his superiors. He must be able to expect a reasonable hearing for his explanation of discrepancies above or below his forecast.

This crisis of confidence affects the 'establishment view' of the process of drawing up budgets as well. If the establishment is the upper limit above which one is rarely, if ever, allowed to go, and if, furthermore, being below establishment is regarded as a saving and therefore laudable, there is an incentive to try to get your own establishment as high as possible. No thought now of making a reasoned stab at what you will actually need: if you set your submission to the manpower budget high, you may actually be able to earn yourself congratulations for not using it all. This often leads managements into a vicious circle of more or less arbitrary cuts in the manpower budget submission. This in turn means that the subordinate manager expects his submission to be cut and he sets it even higher again. He adds on the 5 per cent because he expects that margin of cut. This is compounding the problem.

The solution to this problem is to establish this confidence between board and manager—a particularly difficult thing to do if the problem already exists. As well as making clear what is required, the board must work towards a situation where the manager expects his view to be taken seriously—which implies that he must have a reasoned justification for it—and the board can rely on the manager to present an honest forecast—which implies that they must have a reasoned justification for any modification. These reasoned justifications need the backing of manpower planning techniques. In monitoring manpower, they must seek explanations for being under budget as well as over budget, and take other indicators into account as well as manpower numbers, so that a mere 'on budget' position is not automatically considered good.

The flexible 'rolling plan' approach mentioned in chapter 2 ought to ease this situation by putting the current year's budget in the context of the whole plan, but it is still necessary to ensure that the overstrict establishment view is not taken of Year 1 of the plan, and also to enlist the sensible support of line managers in the forecasting process.

THE ENDURING NATURE OF THE ESTABLISHMENT

In monitoring manpower a view must be taken not only of the comparison of actual manpower with the budget, but also of the comparison of actual output (for example) with that assumed in the budget. If external circumstances have changed markedly, being 'on budget' may be wrong and being under or over budget may be right. In a sophisticated system, one can imagine the use of a computer model to check this. In most, more primitive situations, this is a management judgment.

If being on budget is not necessarily right (though it carries a presumption that it is, unless the opposite can be shown), it is equally true that an establishment for a unit does not necessarily always remain right. Apart from the obvious point that the demands placed on the unit—in effect, the output—may vary, the standards should probably improve: increased productivity was a part of the demand forecast. Yet there is in many establishment control systems a requirement to justify only changes from the establishment (and changes are nearly always upwards in such systems). Surely a retention of the same establishment requires justification; and, if there is a change requested of, say, two more posts, it is not the reason for two more posts which should be sought, but the reason for the total manpower, now perhaps 114 instead of 112. The Royal Air Force, for example, recognising this particular problem, has a team who visit stations to check that current establishments are right, whether or not a change is proposed.

Such an approach may be necessary in so large an organisation but it is bound to be unpopular. In a smaller organisation it is the departure of 'establishment' and the arrival of 'budgets', realistically monitored, that is needed to arrive at the required position of mutual confidence. The reasoned discussion of manpower plans in advance also has all the advantages of a target-setting approach to management, including the commitment of the subordinate manager to the finally approved plan.

VACANCY MARGINS

There is one specific point about manpower numbers which needs to be appreciated and accommodated in the system finally adopted, and that is the vacancy margin. In any 'establishment system' there is an additional reason why the establishment will never be reached. At any particular time there will be some posts in some units unfilled because the job occupant has left and his replacement has not started. This vacancy margin is a function of the labour turnover rate, the length of notice and the length of time taken to recruit staff: all of these will vary with the type of job.

The vacancy margin can be allowed for in the budget by setting the numbers at those likely to be needed after allowing for the vacant posts. However, while this may appear sensible when the company as a whole is taken, it presents problems when it is broken down into comparatively small units. In theory, their vacancy margin may be a fraction of a man-year, so that their manpower budget would not be a whole number (it is difficult to call a manager to task for not employing 15·8 men). In practice, they probably really need 16 men, but muddle along for a couple of months, if they are unlucky enough to lose one of them, whilst another is recruited.

Possibly the best solution is to build up the manpower budget from its component units without allowing for the vacancy margin, but to be aware what it is and take it into account in any global monitoring of the budget. It is, of course, also worth noting variations in the vacancy margin as a measure of recruitment effectiveness and recruitment problems.

Such a solution naturally requires a realistic budget. In the 'establishment' situation, there are likely to be two vacancy margins—the one which appears in the monitoring (the establishment less the actual numbers) and the real margin (the posts actually being filled), which is likely to be a lower figure, and which does not appear from the figures at all. Possibly an even better solution is to use the 'real margin' itself. As has been pointed out, even a realistic budget may be wrong: the true guide to the vacancy margin is the number of replacements being sought at a given time. Planned new posts are not to be included: the point of planning recruitment is that you start the recruitment process before your require the recruit. It may, of course, also be possible to diminish the vacancy margin by anticipating wastage, but this can only be done when the groups of staff are sufficiently large and interchangeable.

CONTROL

The logic of the budgeting method is that an over budget or under budget position is justified after the event. This might be regarded as the 'pure' system. However, there is in fact a difference between the two positions. Whilst in the long term being over budget or under budget can have serious results, as long as monitoring is done at fairly frequent intervals, being over budget is the more serious because it is, except in some fairly unusual circumstances, more difficult to correct. One can mount a recruitment campaign to come up to requirements, but no company can contemplate sackings or redundancies just after recruitment. Therefore a hybrid system may be necessary. Prior approval to go over budget may be required, but to ensure the system works it is necessary not to be excessively restrictive about granting it. Subsequent justification may be used for the under budget situation, but it is extremely important not to neglect this.

The method of presenting the information is important and some form of graphical presentation has much to commend it. This gives the overall picture which can then lead to specific enquiries, and the need for greater detail, with which the personnel director, or whoever else is responsible, would be armed. Figure 9.1 shows a chart used in one

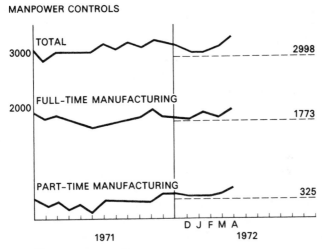

FIG. 9.1   Manpower controls

STAFF STRENGTH REPORT

MONTH 6   YEAR 1970/1

ORGANISATION	PLANNED STRENGTH	ACTUAL STRENGTH	VARIANCE FROM PLAN + or –	VARIANCE AS % OF PLAN + or –	VARIANCES End of quarter			
					1	2	3	4
Division A	2 200	2157	−33	−1·4	−12	−33		
Division B	1 700	1750	+50	+2·9	+60	+50		

FIG. 9.2.   Strength return by computer

company for this purpose, whereas Figure 9.2 shows a simple computer print-out, which avoids presenting too much information in one table: for both there would be back-up detail available but not normally presented.

MONITORING

As well as a control mechanism, the comparison of actual numbers with budget provides a continuous assessment of the forecast and a means of analysing in what respect the forecast was wrong and why.

It is useful not only to make the numerical comparison, which will probably be subdivided into manpower categories, but also to check on the process of the various plans for recruitment, training and so on. The fact that there is a basis in the plan allows these assessments very quickly to make the adaptations to plans occasioned by changing circumstances.

It may be that there are particular elements in the plan which require monitoring on some sort of graphical or statistical basis. An area of concern is quite likely to be productivity, the progress of which forms part of the manpower plan, but which is of obvious importance whether or not there is a plan. Analysis of productivity is also a prerequisite of the manpower demand forecast and as such has been discussed in chapter 3.

MEASUREMENT OF PRODUCTIVITY

When the manpower forecast is being made, the emphasis is on the 'partial' measurement of productivity—the manpower to output relationship. At the stage of monitoring, the manpower planner will be interested in comparing actual events with the forecast, but the company's management is likely to be more interested in overall progress of productivity, taking all relevant factors into account. This wide concept of productivity goes beyond the needs of manpower planning but it is worth examining some of the problems involved so that the distinction between partial and more complete productivity measures is appreciated. A number of studies give greater detail [2].

The major problem is that to measure productivity as a whole one must reduce a variety of outputs to some form of common measure and a variety of inputs to a common measure also. Only then can a productivity ratio be arrived at and monitored over time or compared with a similar ratio for another plant.

The reduction of output to a common measure can be achieved in a number of ways. The use of a 'standard product' is one method. Similar products are related to one particular product, usually the predominant one, as some multiple of it, on some more or less reasoned basis. Another method is to reduce all outputs to monetary value, on the basis of their selling prices in the base year, or of an index of prices (which is really the same thing). Alternatively, output can be measured in terms of production cost, rather than selling price, in the base year, if the production cost for the various items can be arrived at: this overcomes the problems of differing profit margins for different products. Yet another approach is to evaluate the input required for a particular level of production at different times, or places: this, of course, requires an ability to apportion costs.

In calculating output by these measures, allowance must be made for changes in work-in-progress and finished stock; for changes in quality; and for new products, either by calculating or estimating a base year value or by excluding inputs for the new products until a new base year. Similarly, all subsidiary activities (transport, construction etc.) must be specifically included in or excluded from, inputs and outputs.

Inputs must also be reduced to a common measure. One possibility is that of 'imputed man-hours': the value of all inputs is divided by the typical hourly wage. The converse is to translate all into costs, at base year values: each category of manpower, each type of material, each service used and the capital input. Alternatively, the cost of materials and services directly related to a product, instead of being added to the input, can be deducted from the output, so that one is left with the 'added value'.

Thus, total productivity is given by the formula

$$\text{Total productivity} = \frac{V}{M + Q + C}$$

where V = sales volume = value of output
$\quad M$ = input of manpower (in money or man-years)
$\quad Q$ = input of materials (in money or man-years equivalent)
$\quad C$ = input of capital equipment.

The added value method of measuring productivity is

$$\text{Added value} = \frac{V - Q}{M}, \text{ i.e. added value per man}$$

or

$$\frac{V-Q}{M+C}$$

If the concern of management is the use of manpower, then the added value per man will be a useful measure to monitor progress. Since values will all be expressed in base year costs, that is, in a constant way, it might also provide a way of analysing manpower in the past as the basis for forecasting requirements. Furthermore, manpower utilisation and plans for its improvement can be readily understood in the terms of this measure by management, thus providing a helpful way of translating the targets of management into the forecasts of the manpower planner.

The evaluation of capital input is difficult, but important: equipment, stocks, land and buildings and liquid resources should be included. Basically, the approach is to value these at base year prices and apply the base year rate of return. Equipment in most methods must have depreciation applied—at a realistic rate. Land and buildings may be irrelevant if they are unchanged, but if new land or buildings are used, clearly the effect of this is important. Stocks can be significant, because savings can be achieved by reducing stocks held: allowance may be needed for any write-off of stock.

Partial indices, such as output per man, do not take into account the value of all the other inputs to the productive process, whereas these methods of tackling overall productivity do. A defect remains, however, because the inputs are evaluated in terms of base year costs, whereas the relative costs may, in fact, vary. Therefore, although the overall index will in one sense indicate progress, it will not indicate that the 'mix' in the use of resources should have been varied because, for example, money became dearer during the period by a greater amount than the other outputs. This problem is eased if a moving weighting system is used, i.e. if weights always refer to the previous year rather than a particular base year, as suggested in a study of a 'global productivity index' by Électricité de France [3].

MANPOWER COSTS

The importance of costing the various manpower strategies in drawing up the manpower plan has been mentioned. To do this thoroughly it is important to carry out an analysis of what the costs are. Too often these are hidden in various budgets. For example, the cost of recruitment is made up of advertising costs, including the abortive advertisements, and interviewing expenses (both of which are probably separately accounted for in the company's accounting system); but it also includes the personnel officer's time, not forgetting the interviews of those he turned down, his secretary's time in making the arrangements and the materials which she used, the manager's time in discussions with the personnel officer and in interviewing and the induction course. Not all of these are even in the personnel department's budget.

As well as being an analysis that is needed to make proper manpower plans, this is an area which may well be worth monitoring. A working party of the Manpower Society has been studying an approach to this subject.

Figure 9.3 shows the checklist devised by this working party [4]. It can be used just as a checklist for a study of manpower costs, or a section of them, at a point in time. Such a study can be helpful in deciding on manpower policies, as well as costing them realistically in the manpower plan. K. R. Allen and K. G. Cameron have described such a study at one division of Bestobell Ltd [5]. They showed that the non-salary manpower costs of senior staff was over 78 per cent of salary and over 58 per cent in the case of semiskilled operatives, and this led to policy changes. These costs do not include the basic cost of accommodating the staff. In the past few years, costs of accommodation have risen, and the costs of office accommodation, particularly in London, have risen astronomically: between 1968 and 1970 most rents in London more than doubled and are still increasing. £14 to £15 per sq ft is not a surprising rent and at this rate it can cost over £1,000 p.a. for a company to provide space to put a clerk's desk in. Even in the provinces, at about £3 per sq ft, the cost runs into hundreds of pounds a year.

It would be possible to go further than a special study and monitor such costs on a continuing basis. One way to do this, is to 'dig' for the information 'buried' in the accounts, in Dudley Newton's phrase [6]. He has pointed out that by analysing appropriate cost centres, cost elements in other cost centres and special accounts and then adding to this an evaluation of other items obscured in the accounts, one can arrive at a continuing analysis.

In principle, there is no reason why a coding system of the checklist type should not be built into the accounting system, particularly a computerised one, so that such analyses, as well as the conventional ones, could be produced.

MANPOWER COSTS CHECKLIST

Origin of Costs: A checklist of headings under which costs can arise

1   REMUNERATION
1.1   Salary costs
1.1a   Basic pay
1.1b   Bonus payments
1.1c   Overtime
1.1d   Supplementary payments, e.g. shift pay, dirt pay, etc.
1.1e   Merit awards
1.1f   Temporary replacements for holidays, sickness, etc.
1.2   Direct fringe benefits
1.2a   Car
1.2b   Pension fund contributions
1.2c   Luncheon vouchers/subsidised meals
1.2d   Educational support for children of employees
1.2e   Subscriptions to professional bodies
1.2f   Subsidised housing including loans at preferential rates, special mortgages
1.2g   Subsidised travel via loans to buy cars, etc.
1.2h   Season ticket loans
1.2i   Share ownership schemes
1.2j   Location/assignment weighting
1.2k   Holiday — statutory
                — personal days
                — sabbatical
                — other discretionary paid vacation
1.3   Statutory costs
1.3a   National Insurance contributions
1.3b   Graduated pension contributions
1.3c   Selective Employment Tax (regional and industrial payments must be offset against this)
1.3d   Training board contributions (offset by grants, see section 3)
1.3e   Employers' liability
1.3f   Other statutory levies

2   RECRUITMENT COSTS — applicable to avoidable and unavoidable turnover as well as to new jobs
2.1   Pre-recruitment
2.1a   Preparation of review of specifications for both the job to be done and the person to be recruited
2.1b   Briefing of personnel officer (and advertising staff) with line manager
2.1c   Preparation of recruitment programme
2.2   Search
2.2a   All indirect promotional/advertising effort directed at furthering recruitment
2.2b   All direct promotional/advertising effort directed at furthering recruitment including job advertising, stationery, postage, documentation of recruitment records and related administration costs
2.2c   Head hunting costs
2.3   Candidate evaluation
2.3a   Interviewing including travelling, hospitality and the university/college round
2.3b   Bought in selection costs
                — briefing
                — advertising
                — preliminary selection
                — complete selection
2.3c   Selection tests either bought or created and including costs of subsequent administration
2.4   Induction
2.4a   Inducement to move
2.4b   Medical examination prior to establishment procedure
2.4c   Orientation

3   TRAINING COSTS — offset by grants
3.1   Induction period
3.2   Remuneration of trainee and trainer
3.3   Expenses of trainee and trainer including travel and subsistence
3.4   Books and materials used
3.5   Machines and buildings used in continuous training
3.6   Bought out training — school, college, government training centre fees
3.7   Development and maintenance of training programmes

FIG. 9.3   Manpower costs checklist
(reproduced from *Personnel Management*, June 1970)

MANPOWER COSTS CHECKLIST (continued)

including cost of staff in training departments when not actually engaged in direct training

3.8 Reports, appraisal costs of those people other than the trainee and trainer, e.g. counselling reviews

3.9 Training for retirement

3.10 Assimilation costs — the costs incurred of employing a person after induction but before he/she is fully proficient

3.11 Higher material wastage until trainee is fully experienced

3.12 Loss of possible production from trainer whilst he/she is engaged in training

4   RE-LOCATION COSTS — temporary and permanent

4.1 Hostel charges — long term

4.2 Hotel charges — short term

4.3 Direct disturbance allowance

4.4 Costs of disturbance, e.g. legal fees, removal costs

4.5 Premiums paid with regard to housing price differentials or house purchase assistance

4.6 Temporary travel subsidy

4.7 Travelling expenses

4.8 *Ex gratia* re-equipment costs incurred in moving house

5   LEAVING COSTS

5.1 Loss of production between loss and recruitment

5.2 Statutory Redundancy Payments (less rebates)

5.3 *Ex gratia* payments

5.4 Retirement payments (other than pensions)

5.5 Liquidation of direct fringe benefits — could be plus or minus costs

(Note: Leaving may give rise to Recruitment and Training Costs, and sections 2, 3 and 5 should be considered together when considering cost of voluntary turnover)

6   SUPPORT COSTS

6.1 House magazine

6.2 Social club

6.3 Subsidy for other social activities

6.4 Medical welfare schemes

6.5 Canteens

6.6 Safety facilities

6.7 Long service awards

6.8 Suggestion schemes

6.9 Music-while-you-work

6.10 Security service

6.11 Schemes for preferential purchase of goods including costs in purchasing department

6.12 Insurance premiums

6.13 Library and information services

6.14 Use of firms resources for private ends (whether acknowledged or illicit)

6.15 General travel and entertaining expenses not specifically allocatable to a project

6.16 General background training not specifically allocatable to the job being done

6.17 Prestige accommodation

6.18 Car park costs

6.19 Death benefits

6.20 Rehabilitation/convalescent homes

6.21 Holiday homes

7   PERSONNEL ADMINISTRATION

7.1 Organised manpower records — these could be in more than one location in a company with decentralised company activities
These records include:

7.1a Personal record cards

7.1b Personal files

7.1c Salary administration records

7.1d Job specifications

7.1e Manpower planning record

7.2 Salary review costs

7.3 Maintenance of industrial relations including consultative committees

7.4 Manpower research project costs

(The checklist has been drawn up by the Manpower Society.)

Salary and wage costs

On the face of it, salary and wage costs are the easiest element in this costing exercise. These are actual amounts, readily totalled (though probably not in appropriate categories) in the accounting system. However, when one comes to predicting manpower costs, they can become a more difficult element.

Naturally, there is the normal need to predict their ordinary inflation. It is worth remembering here that wage costs rise more quickly, in normal times, than the general run of costs. One has only to look at the average earnings index against the retail price index to see this happening. Various ways can be used to predict the changes, but 'naïve extrapolations' of the rate of rise in the average earnings index or the average earnings in the company itself (if these data are available) might suffice. One can imagine an input from industrial relations experts and salary administrators here.

The 'mix' of manpower may change and affect future costs, but if one is costing a forecast made by manpower categories, this will automatically be taken into account.

For salaried staff, the incremental or progress by merit system is a complicating factor. The cost of manpower is a function of the length of service in a grade and/or the 'merit' of the individuals involved. Brian Wheeler and Peter Andrews have described a way of predicting salary costs in B.P. Ltd. [7]. Their model uses an age structure by category basis as an approximation, reasonable in a career industry, of service in category. The model can then be used to examine the cost effect of different growth rates, of 'status drift'—the tendency to increase the proportion in higher grades—and of different intake patterns.

Human resource accounting

Having costed salaries and the associated costs, we may think we have completed the costing task. But it is necessary for the decision-making process, which essentially involves deciding between alternatives, to consider how these costs should be treated. For, according to accountancy conventions, equipment purchased, which may save on manpower costs, will be capitalised, but the alternative manpower costs will not. The clearest example of a manpower cost which is closely parallel to investing in equipment is training costs. 'Investment' in management training is made to gain in the better use of human resources in the future. The return on this investment is certainly not expected to be received all in one year; yet, that is how the costs involved are charged.

One element of human resource accounting—which sets up new accounting conventions for manpower—is the capitalisation of such costs [8]. The system is in operation at the R. G. Barry Corporation of Columbus, Ohio. The adoption of such a convention helps with understanding the significance of labour turnover as well; for premature leaving means writing off any investment which has taken place. In principle this is the same as writing off a piece of equipment which is badly damaged in some way, though the frequency with which it happens is rather greater. This is balanced by the different relationship between the capital cost (cost of acquisition, training and development, including salary during training) and of 'maintenance' (salary, fringe benefits etc.) from that which applies to machinery.

The depreciation rate of the human resources can be based on 'maximum life', i.e. to retirement, or a more realistic 'expected life', which is a judgment based on past evidence, just as is the depreciation rate of machinery. The effect is to provide at any time an evaluation of the human assets of the company, alongside the other assets. This creates a different conceptual approach to manpower, amongst management, directors and, indeed, shareholders, which, albeit indirectly, is beneficial to those concerned with planning manpower resources. In their turn, the proper evaluation of the capital inputs and of the depreciation period would depend respectively on studies of the manpower costs kind and on studies of manpower retention.

10

Installing manpower planning

'The purpose of planning is to make things change. It must expose the
consequences of doing nothing, show what must be done and awake the
will to get it done.' Sir Harry Douglass (now Baron Douglass of
Cleveland) summed up the virtues—and the problems—of manpower
planning and other forms of planning in 1964. We have already shown
the crucial role of top management in planning decisions because in
these decisions is the meeting point of a number of functions. Perhaps
just as crucial is top management support for the idea of planning
manpower at all, because the manpower planner interacts with all
sorts of people in other functions in doing his job. Without top management's backing his task is more difficult; so that, ideally, he wants top
management agreement before he begins. If he does begin without
explicit support he cannot, of course, continue without their involvement; for it is they who must take the decisions that make things change.

THE ORGANISATIONAL PLACE OF MANPOWER PLANNING

Manpower planning may stem from the top management level. It
may be, on the other hand, that it stems from their advisers. But who
is to do it? In one sense, it does not really matter. The decisions are
management's anyway: the manpower planner merely provides the
data. However, this is obviously a rather naïve view. Minor decisions
are, in fact, taken at a lower level, and a suitable structure must ensure
that these decisions are taken in the right context. They are, even the
minor ones, company decisions: therefore they should be taken within
the structures of the normal functions of the company. Even the minor
ones can have significant effects: therefore, they should be taken at the
suitable hierarchical level. Thus manpower planning is not the task of
a small, specialist, advisory team: it is part of the normal work of the

company. Furthermore, the decisions are about manpower: this at least suggests that it is a part of the personnel function.

In an article already quoted, A. R. Smith [1] has said that historical accident has been at least partially responsible for variations in the location of responsibility for manpower planning. In some firms, it has been left to the line managers, without effective coordination. It has already been argued that the line manager has a major role in short-range manpower planning, but much less in longer range plans, and that, even in the short range, he requires the back-up of information about manpower.

'In others it was viewed simply as a branch of corporate planning,' Smith continues. This time it is the long-range planning which predominates. Certainly, there are extremely strong interconnexions between corporate planning and long-range manpower planning. But, to link the two in one unit, risks losing the close connexion with the shorter range work.

'Some firms regarded it as a financial function.' Again, we have shown how close is the link with financial budgets, but this restricts us to the short-term plan, and endangers the link with the long-term. In some companies, however, long-term and short-term financial planning are located in the finance department, so that this danger is avoided. It leaves the emphasis on finance.

'Some other organisations considered it a mainly "back-room" function to which the operational research or management services unit might be invited to pay attention from time to time.' This hardly needs comment, in view of the emphasis placed on continuing, top level decision-making, though this is not to say that such units should not be involved in establishing the techniques; but it is a part of their role to move on to other things and someone must operate what they have devised.

Finally, let us look at the information used for manpower planning and the sort of plans made. The manpower forecasts require data on categories of manpower, on labour turnover, on transfers and on promotions. The source of this data is the personnel record system: it may need redesigning to be usable, but the information is there. Job descriptions and job analysis may have a role to play in categorising manpower. Staff appraisal may provide useful information on the viability of future career patterns. Salary administration may provide career information also, and certainly can provide financial information.

The plans from the manpower planning process also concern personnel management. Training plans are obviously dependent on future manpower needs. Recruitment plans bear on a major personnel role. Career plans link back to manpower development, appraisal and salary administration, as do plans for improved manpower utilisation: incentive schemes might be appropriate, for example. Trade union negotiations might be relevant to improved utilisation, and certainly will be to redundancy plans. Communications and consultation are important in such situations and may be significant in the retention of manpower. Finally, the monitoring and control of manpower is an area where the personnel manager normally at least provides the information.

So many are the links with personnel management, that there is a very strong case for placing manpower planning in the personnel function. Looked at from the point of view of the personnel manager (and with acknowledgement of the bias of an author who is a personnel manager), virtually all his work is linked to manpower planning and, if he is not responsible for it, he is liable to control not by his management, but by another specialist function. Furthermore, manpower planning provides the means of making his work compatible with—indeed, part of—management objectives. The personnel manager cannot afford not to be involved in manpower planning.

The greatest bar to this is the notorious failure of personnel managers to be numerate. The illogical distinction between the statistical treatment of manpower and a concern with them as human beings tends to reinforce this situation. Yet, nearly all advances in real knowledge, as opposed to intuitive appreciation, in personnel management require a measure of understanding of statistics. Behavioural science may be characterised as 'qualitative', but its results depend on quantification. Factor analysis, sampling, correlation and regression analysis are needed to understand selection tests, attitude studies, group behavioural studies and so on. If the personnel manager is to be more than a spectator of progress in knowledge, he needs more than a mere appreciation. Therefore it is not just manpower planning which demands an increase in numeracy amongst personnel managers[2].

Thus it is suggested that a suitable arrangement is for responsibility for manpower planning to be vested in the personnel function. In a small organisation this may mean one manpower planner or a small group, carrying out all the aspects of the work. In a large organisation, a central team might coordinate all the work of manpower planning but concentrate on developing techniques and on drawing up the long-range plan, whereas the short-range plan would devolve upon the divisional managers, supported with information and advice from their own personnel managers.

The final organisational position of manpower planning mentioned by Smith is 'left to the personnel manager and regarded as no concern of the line manager'. But the line manager is necessarily involved, particularly in the short range planning. The management accountant is involved in the budget–manpower plan link (and may not see why the manpower planner should be interfering in 'his' budget). The corporate planner is involved in long range plans and there is an interaction between his work and the manpower planner's. The other personnel staff are involved, too, in providing data and in putting plans into effect. The cooperation of all must be obtained for fully effective manpower planning. Above all, because of their involvement as well as their backing when the interchange with other functions begins, top management's support is needed.

STARTING MANPOWER PLANNING

It is suggested, therefore, that all these people should have explained to them the concept of manpower planning, perhaps on the basis of chapter 2. It may be that there is a particular aspect of the company which calls for particular attention. The appendix to this chapter sets out a paper to the management of a company (disguised in the appendix) which uses the small profit per employee as a starting point. While it is important to convey the concept of manpower planning as a total system, with all the interactions with other systems, it may be relevant to select one particular project which has an obvious importance to the company and propose this as a first example of manpower planning. Naturally, one must be sure that data exists to tackle the problem and reasonably sure that analysis will reveal a solution. Safer, and having more impact, is the course of presenting a project report as part of the initial educational process, but the prior work involved may not be practicable.

Even if this process of informing those involved goes smoothly, there remains the task of setting the programme for manpower planning in motion. If there is a special project of importance, there is a good start. but the total system must be built from it. The data lack will probably loom large, but it will possibly be worth the risk to begin a rudimentary planning procedure, coordinating with the existing budgetary procedure, on the basis of what data there is, but involving line management's

DISCUSSION GUIDE AND REPORT

Manpower Planning Programme

Discussion with_____ Division_____

Manpower Categories
1. What categories do you have?
   Which are of critical importance?

Demand Forecast
2. Possible predictor variables

3. What historic data is there about (a) manpower and (b) other relevant variables? What sort of categories is it in?

4. Are there any existing productivity measures?

Supply Forecast
5. What wastage data is available? In what categories? Over what period? How is it calculated?

6. How is the wastage data collected? Are reasons for leaving established by exit interview? Is it — or could it be made — service specific?

7. What promotion (change of category and change of grade) data is available? Over what period? Is there any suggestion of a slowing down or speeding up of rates of promotion?

8. Is there any data on transfers between Organisations? Are there any regular patterns?

External Supply
9. What are the particular recruitment difficulties? For what type of staff? What are the main recruitment categories?

10. What contracts do you have with local Employment Exchanges, Youth Employment Service, etc.?

DISCUSSION GUIDE AND REPORT (continued)

1970/72 Forecasts
11. What analyses are necessary/possible before 10 April?

12. Is any help needed?

Future Forecasts
13. What investigations should be set up (with what help)? What data is needed which is not already kept?

Organisation Staff
14. Who will be responsible for manpower analyses? What is his knowledge of manpower planning? What are his training needs?

FIG. 10.1   Discussion guide and report

views as well. In this way a start can be made on manpower planning, so that data can be built up for a clear purpose and so that at least the coordination of policies will result. This may be regarded as a calculated risk; for forecasts will be especially unreliable. Emphasis must therefore be given to the preliminary informative process, to avoid any extravagant expectations.

It is naturally impossible to provide a blueprint for the introduction of the manpower planning process. It will depend on the circumstances of the firm. Whereas the pattern suggested may be suitable, it is possible that data will allow a longer range forecast to be made and this can then be used as a background to discussions with line managers. Whatever the situation, it is certain that there will be existing procedures for budgeting and perhaps corporate planning, and how manpower planning is to interface with them must be fully discussed with those responsible.

A first step may be to discuss the situation with the line managers involved and Fig. 10.1 gives a 'Discussion guide' which is a checklist of possible topics for discussion. This checklist presupposes a large organisation with a central personnel department and line personnel departments. It could be adapted to the smaller company.

If the 'calculated risk' approach is adopted, a form similar to that in Fig. 10.2 might be used. The manager, on the basis of whatever data

1972/3 BUDGET

MANPOWER PROPOSALS

	a	b	c	d	e
Staff category	Current actual month 6 71/2	Establish-ment month 12 71/2	Forecast month 12 71/2	Proposed strengh month 12 72/3	Proposed changes in 72/3 (d − c) ±

f	g	h	i	j	k
Movements out of categories	Trans-fers out	Wastage	Movements into categories	Trans-fers in	Recruitment
Total losses			Total gains		

$k = e + f + g + h - (i + j)$, where e may be positive or negative

FIG. 10.2   Initial manpower planning form

is available to him, is asked, in preparing his budget, to forecast his manpower needs by manpower categories. The need to get away from 'establishment' is emphasised by columns b and c. Column c—the forecast strength—is used as the starting point. Changes of category within the division (cols f and i) will be self-balancing. Transfers in and out of the division (cols g and j) may not be. Finally, recruitment is the 'gain' required to restore the unit to its proposed strength after the 'losses' of transfers and wastage. This recruitment (by categories) can then be analysed into *recruit types*, as already discussed, and a rudimentary recruitment plan drawn up.

Some process such as this can also provide the salary budget for incorporation into the financial budget. This may perhaps be drawn up on the basis of actual, individual salaries, which a computerised system could provide. Salary administration would add the level of increases likely to be awarded in the period as well.

The purpose of establishing manpower planning is to fulfil the twin objectives set out in chapter 2—the incorporation of the planning and control of manpower resources into company planning, and the co-ordination of company manpower policies with each other. The direct effect of this will differ in each company's context. If the problem is high labour turnover, the analysis and coordinated planning will help in solving it. If the problem is utilisation, the analysis, target-setting and control can help. Furthermore, all the aspects of personnel management which have a relevance will play their part if the planning is done well.

Manpower planning, therefore, is concerned with improving the effectiveness of manpower and all the policies concerned with manpower. The viability of other plans may—and often do—depend on it. The assessment of company plans cannot properly be made without it. Can companies afford to neglect the resource of manpower ?

Appendix to Chapter 10

A MANPOWER PROGRAMME FOR COMPANY X

This appendix is set out as a complete report to management. Because it is complete and explains in outline the purpose and method of manpower planning, it also serves as a summary of the whole book.

This report shows why manpower planning is necessary (section 1), especially for Co. X (section 2), and what it achieves (section 3). It sets out what manpower planning is (sections 4–7) and proposes a method of applying it to Co. X (section 8), giving the action needed (section 9) and the costs and savings of the programme (sections 10–12).

1. Manpower and company planning

Manpower is a resource. Like financial and material resources, manpower is a necessity for any enterprise. Unlike them, it has been given little planning attention.

Great care is accorded to the planning of finance and its expenditure is controlled by sophisticated budgetary systems. Material resources are planned with care, and production and sales targets are monitored. Comparable systems have not been applied to planning manpower, however, although manpower absorbs over 12 per cent of the revenue expenditure of the Company in terms of remuneration alone. Furthermore, control is exercised at second hand through financial budgets, which tends to disguise the facts of the manpower situation.

This situation is not unique to Co. X. It has been common throughout British industry. It is changing gradually, because:

(a) There have been, and still are, shortages in some skill categories. The notion that manpower need not be planned because it is always available is not true.

(*b*) It has been increasingly obvious that manpower productivity in Britain falls vastly below the standards set by the USA and some other countries, sometimes by as much as 100 per cent.

(*c*) Allied to poor national performance, has been the increasing Government attention to manpower productivity—for example, through the National Board for Prices and Incomes—and associated legislation, such as the Industrial Training Act.

2.   The need of Co. X for manpower planning

There are a number of reasons which make the need for manpower planning especially pressing for Co. X:

(*a*) Figure 10.3 shows that profit per employee fell in 1971/72 to £238 from £350 in the previous year. It also shows some comparisons with other companies which are in some respects similar. Although slightly better than some, Co. X's performance shows the possibility of, and need for, improved productivity.

(*b*) The management development programme makes the planning of managerial manpower imperative. Nothing is more wasteful of company resources nor more demoralising for the staff concerned than to develop them without regard to future requirements.

(*c*) The productivity schemes introduced in the light engineering works require careful target-setting and control if their full potential is to be realised. The targets should be integrated into general company plans.

(*d*) The restructuring after the absorption of Co. Y makes the time suitable for rethinking top management's information and control systems.

(*e*) The evaluation of the effects of the Co. X research effort on future manpower can only be made if current utilisation is known.

3.   The objectives of manpower planning

Against the background of this general need, both at national and at company level, the objectives of a manpower planning programme can be identified.

Manpower planning aims to fill the gap in management's planning and control of resources and thus to avoid shortages and poor utilisation of manpower. Planning resources is not, however, a task which can be done individually for each resource without reference to the others.

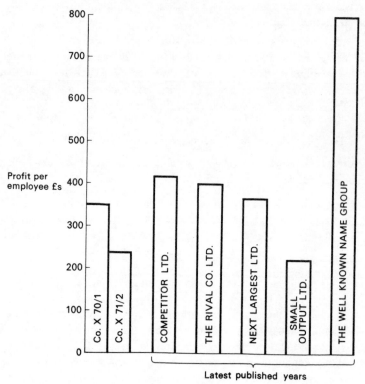

FIG. 10.3   Comparative profits per employee

Manpower costs money and different types cost different amounts. Increased material resources, e.g. machinery, might be a substitute for manpower, and this would involve capital investment. Manpower must be integrated with other planning work. Equally, other planning work is incomplete without manpower planning.

Thus the prime objective of manpower planning is to incorporate the planning and control of manpower resources into company planning.

A second objective is to coordinate manpower policies with each other and with company objectives. Decisions affecting manpower are already being made by line managers and by personnel managers. Recruitment and training programmes, promotion and transfer policies, changes in methods of utilisation or in remuneration, negotiating decisions—all affect the future need for manpower and its supply. At present, such decisions are made in the absence of any clear means of assessing their effects or their relevance to the objectives of the company.

As a result of the achievement of these two objectives, costs are reduced, not only through an overall improvement in productivity, but also through the possibility of giving training, recruitment and the other decisions a clearer direction. In addition, the danger of the company's plans being frustrated through not having the right people at the right place at the right time is obviated. Management control of manpower resources is increased as a result both of the availability of better information and of the systematic use of it.

4.   The manpower planning method

To achieve these objectives, plans for action must be made. These plans are management decisions. However, to be able to make them management requires two forecasts: manpower demand and manpower supply.

In turn, these two forecasts entail a systematic analysis of manpower resources, using current and past data, to provide the means for making projections.

The four elements in manpower planning are thus:

(*a*) Systematic analysis
(*b*) Manpower demand forecast
(*c*) Manpower supply forecast
(*d*) Manpower plans.

5.   Manpower forecasts

The manpower demand forecast derives from the objectives of the company, as Fig. 10.4 shows. The analysis of performance provides the means of translating the objectives into manpower terms. Various techniques are available. They all depend on the analysis of past data, ranging from the derivation of a simple ratio to multiple regression analysis. Even the 'inductive method' of formalising managers' estimates is based on their experience of the past. The method should be selected according to the circumstances and the selection may itself involve some investigation.

Productivity measurement must normally be tackled separately from the analysis of performance, not only because of its special importance, but also because most methods of forecasting manpower demand require modification to allow for improvements in productivity. Methods of productivity measurement also require selection and development according to the circumstances. So that the forecasts are useful in guiding action, they will be divided into cohesive categories of manpower.

The internal manpower supply forecast derives from the analysis of past trends in the retention of labour and of their movements within the company (promotion, change of category and transfer).

The normal method of measuring the wastage of staff is the annual labour turnover index. This measure takes no account of the characteristics of the work force. In particular, length of service, the characteristic found empirically in normal circumstances to have the most significant effect, is disregarded. This defect makes the normal index unsuitable for assessing morale. Totally different leaving patterns can give the same turnover index. It is also unsuitable for forecasting. The trend of the index is meaningless because changes over time will be distorted, or even overshadowed, by changes in the length of service distribution.

A method of analysing the retention of staff which takes length of service into account and which can be used for assessing morale and for forecasting has, therefore, been devised. This 'retention profile' method avoids the data collection problems of more sophisticated methods, but is expected to give an acceptable degree of accuracy. A computer program will be written to make the forecasting calculations based on the profile, taking transfers and changes of manpower category into account.

As shown in Fig. 10.4, the inventory of staff is translated by means of these analyses, into the internal supply forecast.

6.   Reconciliation of forecasts

Normally, recruitment will be necessary to match demand and supply. To plan recruitment an external supply forecast is needed, taking account as far as possible of the total numbers and the probable demand for them from other employers.

The reconciliation must also be achieved within constraints imposed by the budget. This, like the demand forecast, stems from the company plan. It may be, however, that the manpower implications of the company plan are found, when the detailed work has been done, not to be wholly compatible with the financial implications. It may be that financial restrictions limit manpower. In any case, the cost of manpower, and of the plans to supply, develop and retain employees, is an element

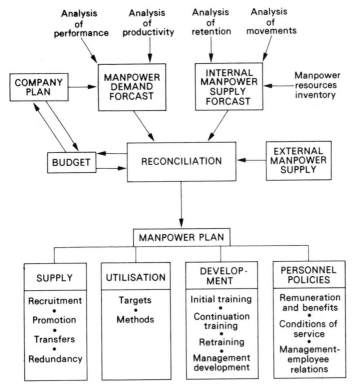

FIG. 10.4   Co. X. manpower planning programme

within the budget itself. Thus, the manpower planning process provides an input to the budgeting process. Because manpower planning both provides an input to the budget and is constrained by it, it is essential that financial and manpower planning be integrated with each other. When the best means of reconciliation are decided, the actions entailed form the manpower plan. In this way, the planning and control of manpower resources is incorporated into company planning, which is the first objective of the programme.

7.   The manpower plan

The manpower plan has four elements:

(a) *Supply.* Recruitment programme, including anticipated problems; promotion policy, including the effect on morale of changes policy on transfers between companies within Co. X; if necessary, redundancy programme. Such measures affect supply.

(b) *Utilisation*. Targets for improved productivity (which cannot be set until productivity can be measured), including means of achieving them. This would affect demand.

(c) *Development*. Initial training for recruits; continuation training; improving productivity, preparing for promotion and transfer; retraining. Management development would be absorbed into this part of the programme.

(d) *Personnel policy*. Most other aspects of personnel policy have a bearing on manpower supply, affecting both the ability to recruit and to retain staff. Remuneration and benefit policies and conditions of service are clearly relevant. The retention of staff is also dependent on the atmosphere created for them by management. The manpower planning process can demonstrate the urgency of changes concerning these management/employee relations. Considerations of manpower demand and supply are relevant also to negotiations about pay and conditions. Furthermore, the fact that the company is known to think ahead about its manpower could well increase the unions' confidence in it.

These four elements of the manpower plan show how personnel policies are coordinated with each other and with the company's objectives, which is the second objective of the programme.

8. The Co. X programme

Manpower planning will be divided into two parts:

(a) short-range: two years ahead;
(b) long-range: five years ahead.

Short-range planning is concerned with the tactical questions of planning and personnel activities, e.g. recruitment and training. Line personnel managers are vitally concerned and will themselves carry out the analyses, enabling line managers to make the planning decisions. A central department would offer specialist advice and assistance with techniques, and provide relevant information, e.g. on labour market trends. This department, working with the Budgets department, would also consolidate forecasts into a company plan. Long-range planning is concerned with strategic issues. It is less detailed and is linked closely

with company planning advice to the board. Theref re, it will be carr
out by the central department, in conjunction with company planne.
The two parts of the programme are nevertheless interdependent. Th
long-range forecasts provide background for the short-range. The short-
range exercise will build up data required for long-range.

9. Action programme

(a) Set up manpower planning department within Central Personnel

Apr./Sept. 72

(b) Devise programme and explain to line managers   Sept. 72/Jan. 73

(c) Simplified forecasts made for 1973/74   Feb./Aug. 73

(d) Train line personnel staff   Feb/Sept. 73

(e) Develop short-range forecasting techniques and associated data
collection   May 73/Feb. 74

(f) Begin long-range studies   May 73

10. The cost of the programme

An estimation of the cost of the programme is given below in Section 11
and amounts to £47,000 p.a.

The benefits of achieving the objective of improved strategic planning
are incalculable. Benefits at the tactical level themselves would easily
save the cost of the programme. Some examples are given in Section 11.

11. Cost estimates

Since a first step in manpower planning is to assess the viability of
different forecasting methods and since those examined first may or
may not prove satisfactory, it is impossible to lay down with exactitude
how much effort is required to set up a system. However, experience has
shown that, very roughly, a half man-year p.a. for two years is required for
a thorough examination of an organisation of about 3,500. Subsequently, the workload might fall. Thus, the cost during the earlier
years of the programme might be:

(a) *Work of line personnel staff*
roughly, half man-year for each 3,500 = 9
man-years (Some work, e.g. on labour
turnover, is already done, but not applied
to forecasting.)

£2,500 per man-year		£22,500

(b) *Central manpower unit*

	approx. rates
Manager	£5,000
Secretary	£1,500
Statistician	£2,500
Personnel Officer	£2,000
Clerk (or possibly trainee)	£1,500
	£12,500

(c) +20 per cent on salaries for benefits etc.	£7,000
(d) Computer time, revised data recording systems etc. + some managerial time	£5,000
	£47,000

12. Savings

Savings also cannot be exactly calculated, because analysis is required—indeed, is designed—to discover what improvements can be made. They could, however, be far in excess of the cost. Even if the only benefit were coordination of existing personnel activities with the company objectives, the cost would be quickly recovered, for example, through reducing misdirected training or recruitment efforts. Some examples of possibilities show just how little the cost of manpower planning is:

(a) A saving of 44 men at the average salary (£1,070 p.a.) would cover the cost. This is less than 0·07 per cent of the work force.
(b) The cost would be covered by a fractional increase in productivity, about 0·01 per cent (which would increase turnover by about £45,000).
(c) The cost of labour turnover (recruitment costs, lost production etc.) is approximately £120 per leaver. A reduction in the percentage annual labour turnover of 0·6 would cover the cost.

(*d*) If management trainees are not geared to future needs and 12 too many are recruited in a year, the cost might be about £4,000 each in salary and recruiting costs (for a two-year traineeship), amounting to more than the cost of planning.

Any one of these benefits would pay for the manpower planning programme. Its effect in providing data for better informed, top management decisions could be far greater. It could be seen as an insurance against the misutilisation of one of the company's resources at a premium of only 0·03 per cent of profit.

References

Chapter 1. The rise of manpower planning

[1] WILLIAM ALLEN. 'Half-time Britain', *Sunday Times*, 1 March 1964.
[2] KEITH RICHARDSON. 'Make or break for half-time Britain', *Sunday Times*, 2 January 1972.
[3] *The National Plan*, HMSO, 1965.
[4] MINISTRY OF LABOUR. *The Pattern for the Future*, Manpower Studies no. 1, HMSO, 1964.
[5] *The Metal Industries*, Manpower Studies no. 2, 1965.
The Construction Industry, Manpower Studies no. 3, 1965.
Computers in Offices, Manpower Studies no. 4, 1965.
Electronics, Manpower Studies no. 5, 1967.
Occupational Changes 1951–1961, Manpower Studies no. 6, 1967.
Growth of Office Employment, Manpower Studies no. 7, 1968.
All published by HMSO.
[6] *Ninth Report from the Estimates Committee: Manpower Training for Industry*, HMSO, 1967.
[7] *Review of the Central Training Council*, Cmnd 4335, HMSO, 1970.
[8] DANIEL H. GRAY. *Manpower Planning*, London, Institute of Personnel Management, 1967.
[9] THE EDINBURGH GROUP. *Perspectives in Manpower Planning: an Edinburgh Group Report*, Institute of Personnel Management, London 1967.
[10] DEPARTMENT OF EMPLOYMENT AND PRODUCTIVITY. *Company Manpower Planning*, Manpower Papers no. 1, HMSO, 1968.
[11] C. G. LEWIS ed. *Manpower Plannning: a bibliography*, English Universities Press, 1969.
[12] D. J. BARTHOLOMEW and B. R. MORRIS eds. *Aspects of Manpower Planning*, English Universities Press, 1971.
[13] A. R. SMITH. 'Manpower planning in the management of the Royal Navy', *Journal of Management Studies*, 4, 1967, 127–39.
[14]. W. N. JESSOP, ed. *Manpower Planning: operational research and personnel research*, English Universities Press, 1966.
This reports the 1965 NATO Conference in Brussels. Subsequent conferences are reported as follows:

N. A. B. WILSON, ed. *Manpower Research*. English Universities Press, 1969. (The 1967 conference in London.)

A. R. SMITH, ed. *Models of Manpower Systems*. English Universities Press, 1970. (The 1969 conference in Oporto.)

Chapter 2. Manpower planning in the company

[1] E. F. L. BRECH. *Managing for Revival*, Management Publications Ltd for BIM, 1972.

Chapter 3. Manpower demand forecasts

[1] D. J. BARTHOLOMEW. 'An introduction to concepts and terms' in *Some Statistical Techniques in Manpower Planning*, ed. A. R. Smith, (CAS Occasional Papers no. 15), HMSO, 1970.

[2] ANNE CRICHTON and P. ANTHONY. 'A survey of the role of the personnel specialist in industrial relations' unpublished paper presented to the I.R. Committee of the Institute of Personnel Management in 1968.

[3] K. A. YEOMANS. *Statistics for the Social Scientist*, vol. 1, *Introducing Statistics*; vol. 2, *Applied Statistics*, Penguin Books, 1968.

[4] R. M. CURRIE. *Work Study*, British Institute of Management, London, 1965.

[5] A. R. SMITH. 'Manpower planning in the management of the Royal Navy', *Journal of Management Studies*, **4**, 1967, 127–39.

[6] I. G. HELPS. 'Craft manpower planning at an industry level', unpublished paper read to the Manpower Planning Conference of the OR Society Manpower Planning Study Group, 25 June 1968.

[7] E. J. BROSTER. 'The learning curve for labour', *Business Management*, March 1968, pp. 34–7.

[8] A. J. SIMON. 'The unnecessary mystique surrounding manufacturing progress models', *Journal of Management Studies*, **5**, no. 3, 1968.

Chapter 4. Internal manpower supply forecasting

[1] A. M. BOWEY. 'Labour stability curves and a labour stability index', *British Journal of Industrial Relations*, **8**, no. 1, 1969, 71–83.

[2] ANGELA BOWEY. 'A measure of labour stability', *Personnel Management*, London, **3**, no. 4, April 1971, 26–31.

[3] K. F. LANE and J. E. ANDREW. 'A method of labour turnover analysis', *Journal of the Royal Statistical Society*, Series A, **118**, 1955, 296–323.

[4] H. TORRANCE. *The Prediction of Labour Turnover using a Mathematical Model*, Paper OD(E)/130/OR, Central Electricity Generating Board, 1967.

[5] P. L. ASHDOWN. 'Wastage and turnover', in *Some Statistical Techniques in Manpower Planning*, ed. A. R. Smith (CAS Occasional Papers 15) HMSO, 1970.

[6] D. T. BRYANT. 'A survey of the development of manpower planning policies', *British Journal of Industrial Relations*, **3**, no. 3, 1965, 279–90.

[7] D. J. BARTHOLOMEW. *Stochastic Models for Social Processes*, Wiley, 1967.

[8] ANDREW YOUNG. 'Demographic and ecological models of manpower planning', in *Aspects of Manpower Planning*, ed. D. J. Bartholomew and B. R. Morris, English Universities Press, 1971.

[9] INSTITUTE OF MANPOWER STUDIES. *IMS 72*, 1972.

[10] E. JONES. 'Officer career planning in the Royal Navy', *Operational Research Quarterly*, **20**, 1969, 33 ff.

[11] E. JONES. The paper was published as 'The application of actuarial techniques to officer career planning' in *Manpower Research in the Defence Context*, ed. N. A. B. Wilson, English Universities Press, 1969.

[12] C. W. WALMSLEY. 'A simulation model for manpower planning' in *Manpower and Management Science*, ed. D. J. Bartholomew and A. R. Smith, English Universities Press, 1971.

Chapter 5. External manpower supply

[1] MINISTRY OF LABOUR. *The Pattern of the Future*, Manpower Studies no. 1, HMSO, London 1964. This sets out the assumptions to be made very clearly.

[2] See, for example:
D. BELL and D. COLEMAN. 'Levies, grants and manpower training for industry', *Technical Education and Industrial Training*, **10**, no. 5, 1968, 201–3;
EDINBURGH GROUP. *Perspectives in Manpower Planning*, Institute of Personnel Management, 1967.

[3] *Manpower Training for Industry*: Ninth Report of the Estimates Committee of the House of Commons in Session 1966–67, HMSO, 1967.

[4] *Review of the Central Training Council*, Report of a Committee under the Chairmanship of the Rt. Hon. Frank Cousins, Cmnd 4335 HMSO, 1970.

[5] *Perspectives in Manpower Planning*

[6] SANTOSH MUKHERJEE. *Changing Manpower Needs: a study of Industrial Training Boards*, PEP, 1970.
SANTOSH MUKHERJEE, *Making Labour Markets Work*, PEP, 1972.

[7] *Report into Higher Education*, Committee on Higher Education (Chairman, Lord Robbins), Cmnd 2154, HMSO, 1963.

[8] DEPARTMENT OF EMPLOYMENT. *People and Jobs*, HMSO, 1971.

[9] D. ROBINSON. 'Myths of the local labour market', *Personnel*, **1**, no. 1, 1967.

[10] DAN GOWLER. 'Determinants of the supply of labour to the firm', *Journal of Management Studies*, **6**, no. 1, 1969.

Chapter 6.   The manpower plan

[1] R. W. MORGAN. 'Linear programming in manpower planning', in *Some Statistical Techniques in Manpower Planning*, ed. A. R. Smith (CAS Occasional Paper 15), HMSO, 1970.

[2] D. PYM. 'Technical change and the misuse of professional manpower' *Occupational Psychology*, **41**, no. 1, 1967, 1–16.

[3] *A Review of the Scope and Problems of Scientific and Technological Manpower Policy*, Cmnd 2800, HMSO, London, 1965.

[4] J. W. KUHN. *Scientific and Managerial Manpower in the Nuclear Industry*, Columbia University Press, 1966.

[5] P. R. HODGSON. 'Manpower planning—at the level of the firm' *BACIE Journal*, December 1965, 150–7.

[6] EDINBURGH GROUP. *Perspectives in Manpower Planning*, Institute of Personnel Management, 1967.

[7] *Code of Industrial Relations Practice*, HMSO, 1972.

[8] A. R. SMITH. 'Developments in manpower planning', *Personnel Review* **1**, no. 1, Autumn 1971.

[9] D. J. BELL. 'Pitfalls of manpower planning', *Personnel* **1**, no. 12, November 1968.

[10] JUDITH HOBBS and COLIN LEICESTER. 'Changing patterns in the labour force', *Personnel Management*, **5**, no. 5, May 1973.

[11] R. BRECH. *Britain 1984: Unilever's Forecast*, Darton, Longman & Todd, 1963.

Chapter 7.   A computer model

No references.

Chapter 8.   Data collection

[1] EDGAR WILLE. *The Computer in Personnel Work*, Institute of Personnel Management, 1966.

[2] JOAN SPRINGALL. *Personnel Records and the Computer*, IPM and Industrial Society, 1971.

[3] J. BAYHYLLE and A. HERSLEB. *The development of electronic data processing in manpower areas*, OECD, 1973.

[4] For value of these records, see, for example:
EDINBURGH GROUP. 'How the new Race Act Affects Personnel', *Personnel* **2**, no. 2, February 1969.

[5] INSTITUTE OF MANPOWER STUDIES. *Introduction to IMSSOC*, Institute of Manpower Studies, 1972.

Chapter 9.   Manpower controls

[1] For a discussion of the behavioural problems of budgeting, as well as some means of incorporating manpower data, see:
A. G. HOPWOOD. 'The relationship between accounting and personnel management—past conflicts and future potential', *Personnel Review*, **1**, no. 2, Spring 1972.

[2] T. E. EASTERFIELD. *Productivity Measurement in Great Britain*, Department of Scientific and Industrial Research, 1959.

J. E. FARADAY. *The Management of Productivity*, Management Publications Ltd. for BIM, London, 1971.

J. W. KENDRICK and J. CREAMER. *Measuring Company Productivity*, US National Industrial Conference Board, 1964.

H. SANSBURY. 'The measurement of productivity', *Management Accountant*, October 1966, 389–95.

OECD, *Productivity Measurement*, vols. 1 and 2, Paris, OECD, 1955.

[3] ÉLECTRICITÉ DE FRANCE. 'Les progrès de productivité et leur utilisation a l'Électricité de France de 1952 à 1962', *Études et Conjoncture*, no. 1, 1965.

[4] DENNIS YORK and CAROLYN DOOLEY. 'Checking the manpower costs', *Personnel Management*, **2**, no. 6, June 1970, 34–5.

[5] KEITH R. ALLEN and KEITH G. CAMERON. 'Manpower costing in action', *Personnel Management*, **3**, no. 2, Feb. 1971, 26–9.

[6] DUDLEY NEWTON. 'Structuring the costs for decisions', paper presented to Manpower Society Conference 1971.

[7] BRIAN WHEELER and PETER ANDREWS. 'Cost of an age structure', *Personnel Management*, **4**, no. 5, May 1972, 32–6.

[8] R. L. BRUMMET, W. C. PYLE and E. G. FLAMHOLTZ, eds. *Human Resource Accounting Development and Implementation*, Foundation for Research on Human Behavior, Ann Arbor, Michigan, 1969. Also numerous articles by these authors, e.g. 'Human resource accounting in industry', *Personnel Administration*, July–Aug., 1969.

W. J. GILES and D. F. ROBINSON. *Human Asset Accounting*, Institute of Personnel Management and Institute of Cost and Management Accountants, 1972.

Chapter 10. Installing manpower planning

[1] A. R. SMITH. 'Developments in manpower planning', *Personnel Review*, **1**, no. 1, Autumn 1971.

[2] See, for example, EDINBURGH GROUP. 'A modular approach to training', *Personnel Management*, July 1969.

Index